Acknowledgements

This report draws on a wide range of research carried out in recent years, particularly by the Welfare State Programme at the Suntory and Toyota International Centres for Economics and Related Disciplines at the London School of Economics. This research was supported by Suntory Limited, the Economic and Social Research Council (under programme grant X206 32 2001), the Joseph Rowntree Foundation and others. It also draws on a wide range of research on social policy and housing issues supported by the Joseph Rowntree Foundation at other institutions. The writing of the report itself formed part of the Foundation's Programme on Income and Wealth.

This updated edition was prepared thanks to the great assistance of Karen Gardiner from the Welfare State Programme. While the substance of the report is largely unchanged from its first edition, the statistics it contains have been updated to reflect information available up to June 1997.

The production of this report has been a combined effort by members of the Welfare State Programme, with direct contributions from Jane Dickson, Maria Evandrou, Martin Evans, Jane Falkingham, Howard Glennerster and Julian Le Grand. It draws heavily not only on their research but also that of colleagues, including Tony Atkinson, Nick Barr, Karen Gardiner, Carli Lessof, Holly Sutherland, Polly Vizard and David Winter. Others who have helped greatly in commenting on drafts and in discussions leading to its preparation include Penny Bernstock, Virginia Bovell, John Carrier, Deborah Georgiou, Mark Kleinman, Jane Lewis, David Piachaud, Anne Power, Chris Trinder, Gail Wilson and Christine Whitehead. Thanks are due not only to them, but also to officials of the Departments of Education, Employment, Health, and Social Security who kindly helped provide information and advice, and to the ESRC Data Archive for the supply of GHS and FES microdata analysed by the Welfare State Programme. Interpretation of this information and data is entirely my own responsibility.

Summary

Part 1: Background

Welfare spending

Over the last twenty years or so, Britain's welfare spending has been stable as a share of GDP. That share - about a quarter of GDP - is below that in most other European countries.

There are upward pressures: the ageing population; SERPS; and higher basic pension entitlements. But, even if benefit levels kept up with overall living standards, the total net effects on public finances over the next *fifty* years would add up to an addition of under 5 per cent of GDP - no more than the increase (mainly due to the recession) over the *three* years to 1992.

Aims of the welfare state

The welfare state has much wider aims than just the relief of poverty. These include:
● Insurance of all against risks like illness and unemployment;
● Redistribution towards those with greater needs - such as for medical care, disability, or family circumstances;
● Smoothing out the level of income over the life cycle;
● Stepping in where the family 'fails' - for instance, assisting lone parents.

Analysis of the redistributive effects of the welfare state, taking into account the taxes which finance it, shows that it does redistribute between rich and poor, but it also smoothes out income over the life cycle for people with average incomes, acting as a kind of 'savings bank'. It also has a major effect in evening out incomes between men and women.

Side-effects

Side-effects of welfare provision may deter people from working (the 'unemployment trap' and the 'poverty trap') or from accumulating savings or small occupational pensions (the 'savings trap'). These problems grow more acute the more benefits are 'targeted', particularly through means-testing. The scale of these effects may be limited or unproven, but they may be seen as unfair, bringing the whole system into disrepute.

Social and economic change

Things have changed since Beveridge:
● The population is older;
● Families are less stable and uniform, with greater cohabitation, divorce and lone parenthood;
● Unemployment, female labour force participation, part-time work and self-employment have all grown.

These changes cause problems for a social insurance system originally designed for a labour market dominated by full-time male employee breadwinners. Meanwhile, the *scale* of the problems faced by the welfare state has increased: whatever kind of measuring rod used, the number of people with low incomes increased over the 1980s, substantially so if any measure relative to current living standards is used.

Part 2: Options for reform

Part 2 of the report examines proposals for reform of different parts of the welfare state.

Options discussed include:

- Greater means-testing of social security, including the basic pension;

- Tax-benefit integration and basic incomes;

- The future of the contributory principle;

- Adequacy of benefit levels and uprating policy;

- Policies for getting claimants back into work;

- Pension ages;

- The 'internal markets' in the NHS, education, housing and personal social services;

- Pressures on health costs and responses to them;

- Options for funding higher education;

- Rent policy and the structure of Housing Benefit; and

- Personal sources for funding long-term care.

Part 3: Conclusions

Much current debate starts from the assumption that welfare policy is boxed in by fiscal constraints. This report suggests there is actually a wide range of options, summarised in Figure 51 of the report.

The scale of welfare spending

There is no 'demographic time bomb' which will cause an unsustainable explosion of welfare costs. Although upward pressures on spending will continue, their scale still leaves a real choice about the future of the welfare state:

- We could maintain or even improve provision in relation both to need and contemporary living standards, accepting a slow rise in the share of welfare spending in GDP and hence in the taxes or contributions required to pay for it. The rise implied by maintaining services while the population ages would not take Britain's welfare spending above the share of national income already spent in most other European countries.
- We could keep spending down by continuing to link benefits to prices, not to contemporary living standards. It is questionable whether this is sustainable. Had it been done since 1948, the basic single pension would only be just above £25 per week today, instead of £62.45.
- We could maintain the relative value of certain items but cut out others altogether or narrow the groups covered.

Ways of targeting welfare

The welfare state is already 'targeted' on those with lower incomes. The debate is not about *whether* to target, but *how* to do so. Possible instruments include:

- Provision for needs or contingencies affecting those with low incomes most;
- Financing flat-rate benefits from taxes or contributions which rise with income;

- Means-testing;
- Tax allowances or clawing-back benefits through the tax system.

Whichever form of targeting is used, incentives are affected. The choice is over what form any implied disincentives take.

Paying for welfare

Further choices come in the balance between different ways of paying for public welfare:
- General taxation and public borrowing;
- 'Hypothecated' taxes, earmarked for a particular use;
- Contributions which affect individual benefit rights;
- Charges on users;
- Recovering costs later through some kind of loan.

The system of provision

Recent reorganisation of the welfare services has been aimed at improving their efficiency through devolving decision-making and introducing competition between providers. Some efficiency gains are being realised, but there are costs to running internal markets, difficulties in ensuring equity in treatment and funding arrangements, and in 'empowering' *users*, rather than providers (or professional purchasers).

While the private sector is the most efficient solution in some areas, it is not in others. Public involvement is not only needed to transfer incomes from rich to poor, but also in areas where, left to itself, the market would not produce an efficient solution. There are other areas where state provision, or at least the particular form it takes, can get in the way of private provision.

Beyond welfare

Massive changes to labour markets and family structures are leading to increased inequality, greatly raising the demands made on the welfare state. While policies lying outside 'welfare policy' as narrowly defined may be most critical, the future welfare state must be capable of responding to these challenges.

Introduction

The future of the welfare state is under review. The new Labour Government has embarked on a series of reviews of key spending areas and has pledged itself to produce a 'modernised welfare state'. Shortly before it left office, the Conservative Government had proposed radical reforms to the state pension system. Fundamental questions are being asked about what kind of welfare state Britain should have - and can afford. At the same time, numerous research studies are shedding new light on the operation and effectiveness of welfare services, and many pressure groups and others are putting forward their ideas for reform in particular areas.

The aim of this report is to lay out in accessible form the background to the debate and the key areas where welfare services are under review. It does not set out any kind of blueprint for the future of welfare, but rather provides the information needed to understand the terms of that debate and to put individual proposals and options in context.

The first key issue (examined on pp 8-14) is whether the cost of the welfare state is rising unsustainably, outstripping the nation's ability to pay for it. If so, policy would be boxed in, and restructuring and withdrawal from certain kinds of provision would be inevitable. If not (as that section concludes), we can choose as a nation whether to maintain services or whether to restrict services to keep down taxation to whatever level is judged acceptable.

The next section examines the distributional effects of the welfare state as it is now, measuring these against the varied aims which have been advanced for public welfare provision, aims which go wider than simply the relief of poverty. Is it succeeding in these aims, or is greater 'targeting' in some form needed for it to do so?

This is followed by an examination of the side-effects of welfare provision, particularly on labour market incentives and on saving for retirement (pp 22-29). As well as examining how problems like the 'poverty trap' or the 'savings trap' arise, the section examines their quantitative importance and wider implications.

As the final part of background to the current debate, the next section looks at how the social and economic environment in which the welfare state operates has changed: the ageing population, changing family structures, a changing labour market and, in recent years, a rapid growth in income inequalities and the numbers with low incomes. Even if the structure of welfare services had been ideal for the 1950s or 1960s, these changes raise questions about whether they need now to be adapted to deal with a different world from that envisaged by Beveridge and others fifty years ago.

Part 2 looks in turn at the main welfare services - social security and pensions, health services, education, housing and personal social services - outlining some of the main options for reform advanced in the recent debate, discussing their advantages and drawbacks, and summarising the main choices facing policy-makers.

Finally, Part 3 brings these various strands together, arguing that, far from being boxed in, welfare policy faces a wide range of inter-related options, with similar questions being raised across the welfare services about issues like targeting, financing systems, who should provide publicly financed services, the role of the private sector, and what can be done to reduce the demands placed on the welfare state.

John Hills
London School of Economics
July 1997

Is the welfare state in crisis?

Can we afford it?

Direct government spending on the main welfare services (education, health, housing, personal social services and social security) reached nearly £190 billion in 1996-97.[1] Social security - with pensions the largest single item - represented half the total, and education and health each about one-fifth (**Figure 1**).

Welfare spending was almost two-thirds of all government spending, and over a quarter of national income (GDP). In the three years up to 1992-93, its share of GDP rose from 21.4 to 26.3 per cent, since when it has fallen back.

Tax reliefs given in 1995-96 included £2.8 billion for mortgage interest, £7.5 billion for occupational pension schemes, and £2.1 billion for personal pension schemes. While in each case there is some dispute about how to calculate the precise value of tax concessions,

the 'fiscal welfare state' clearly remains substantial, and has the same effect on government borrowing as the same amount of direct spending.

The long-term picture

Given its rapid recent growth, fears that such spending may "outstrip the nation's ability to pay"[2] are understandable. However, the long-term picture is much less dramatic. **Figure 2** shows that, after reaching over 10 per cent in the early 1930s, the share of national income - which is what matters for our 'ability to pay' - taken by education, health and social security fell back during the War. Then came thirty years of continuous growth as post-War legislation came to fruition, taking the share to 20 per cent by the mid-1970s, after which it levelled out, but with further growth in the early 1990s.

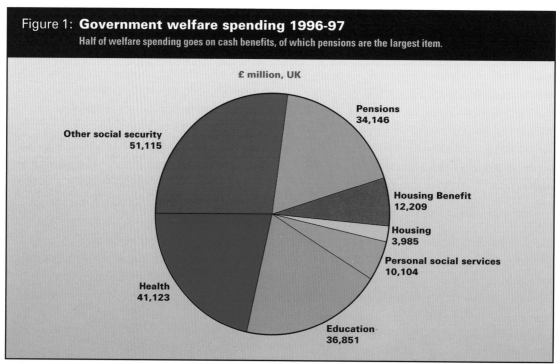

Figure 1: **Government welfare spending 1996-97**
Half of welfare spending goes on cash benefits, of which pensions are the largest item.

£ million, UK

Pensions 34,146

Other social security 51,115

Housing Benefit 12,209

Housing 3,985

Personal social services 10,104

Health 41,123

Education 36,851

Source: HM Treasury (1997)

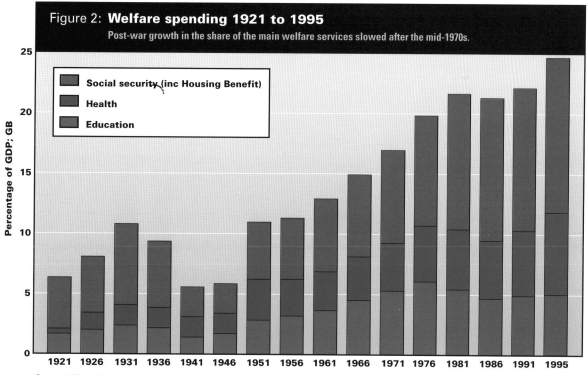

Figure 2: **Welfare spending 1921 to 1995**
Post-war growth in the share of the main welfare services slowed after the mid-1970s.

Source: Hills (1992) updated

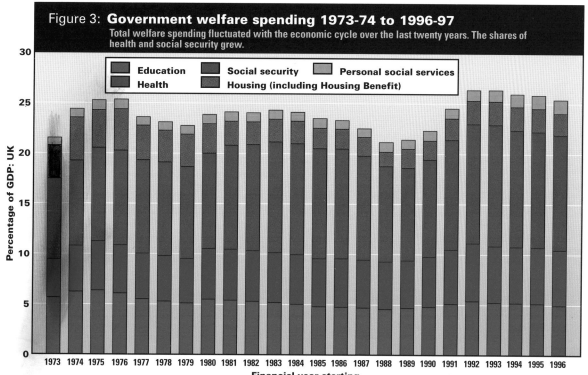

Figure 3: **Government welfare spending 1973-74 to 1996-97**
Total welfare spending fluctuated with the economic cycle over the last twenty years. The shares of health and social security grew.

Source: HM Treasury (1997) and Hills (1990)

The story of the last twenty years is shown in more detail in **Figure 3**, including spending on housing and personal social services. There has been neither inexorable growth nor decline in the relative scale of the welfare state in recent years. The rising share of welfare spending hit a ceiling in the mid-1970s that reflected the oil crisis and the visit of the IMF, and predated the 1979 change of government.

Since then, the total has fluctuated with the economic cycle, with growth in the early 1990s reflecting the depth of the recession - and some relaxation in spending controls before the 1992 election - rather than the medium-term trend. What has changed in the medium term has been the *composition* of welfare spending - away from housing and education, towards social security and the NHS.

International comparisons

This levelling-out in the share of social spending in the economy was not unique to Britain. There was rapid growth in the share of social spending[3] in GDP in most industrialised countries between 1960 and 1981. Since then, the picture has been more mixed, with falls in some countries in the 1980s and slower growth in others. Overall, social spending has grown as a share of GDP, with the unweighted average for the countries shown rising from 25 to nearly 30 per cent, twice as large an increase as in the UK.

Figure 4 also shows that the relative scale of Britain's welfare state is smaller than that of most industrialised countries - thirteenth out of the 19 countries listed in the figures for 1993, down from eleventh out of 18 in 1981. In the European Union, only Portugal, Ireland and Greece had a lower share.

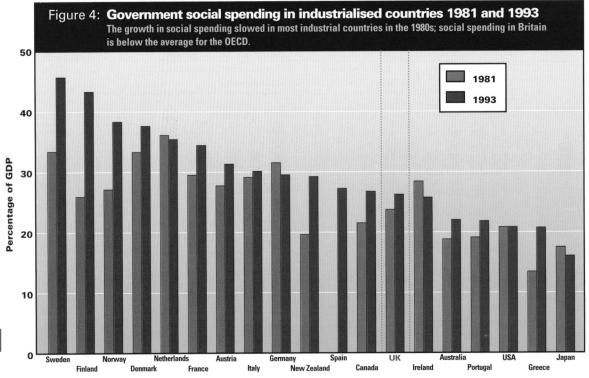

Figure 4: **Government social spending in industrialised countries 1981 and 1993**
The growth in social spending slowed in most industrial countries in the 1980s; social spending in Britain is below the average for the OECD.

Sources: OECD (1985, 1996a, 1996b) UK 1993 figures use social security spending from HM Treasury (1997)
Note: Figures for Australia, New Zealand and Japan use 1992 data.

Pressures from ageing

A second reason for concern about growth in welfare spending is that such spending is particularly focused on older people, and the population is ageing. The bars in **Figure 5** give estimates of how average public spending on people's education, health and social security (including Housing Benefit) varied with age in 1991.

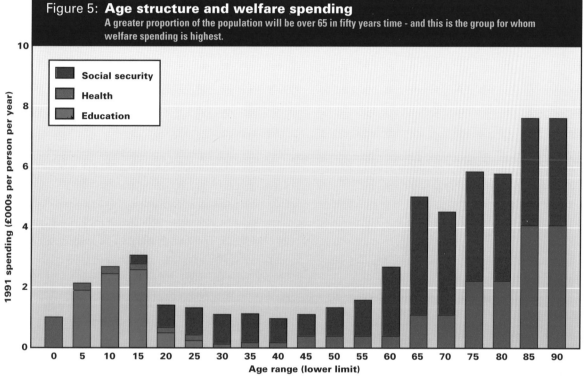

Figure 5: **Age structure and welfare spending**
A greater proportion of the population will be over 65 in fifty years time - and this is the group for whom welfare spending is highest.

Source: Hills (1992) using 'high variation' of health with age

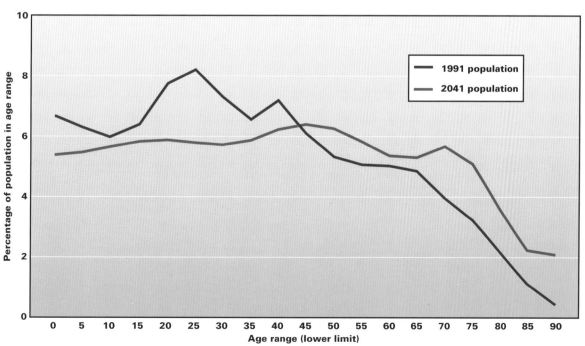

Source: OPCS (1993b)

11

An initial peak of over £3,000 per year in 1991 - mainly from education - is reached at ages 15-19. After that, the total falls back during people's working lives, but both social security and health spending rise rapidly after pension age, reaching more than £7,500 per year for those of 85 or over.

Given this pattern, the age structure of the population is a key determinant of spending. The figure also shows the population structure of Great Britain in 1991 (the orange line), with the proportion in each five-year age group falling quite rapidly from age 70. About 16 per cent of the population was already aged above 64 in 1991, the age group for whom spending is highest. Overall, average spending per head of population on the three services was £2,240 in 1991-92.

The green line shows the forecast age structure of the population in fifty years' time, 2041. The proportion of the population over 65 is forecast to rise to 24 per cent, with the proportion in their nineties nearly quintupling.

Suppose we had the age structure of 2041 today, but spent the same amount on each person of a given age. What would happen to average spending per member of the whole population? Given the older population, it would rise - to £2,600 per member, 17 per cent above actual spending in 1991-92[4] an increase equivalent to 3.8 per cent of GDP at 1991-92 spending levels.

Even if the key determinants of welfare spending - like benefit levels and health workers' salaries - were to be maintained in relation to incomes in general, ageing by itself would therefore imply spending growth at a rate of 0.32 per cent per year over the next fifty years. This may seem surprisingly undramatic, in the light of discussion of "the demographic time bomb".[5] The trends have to be kept in perspective. What tends to be forgotten is that Britain went through the ageing process relatively early, by comparison with other countries.

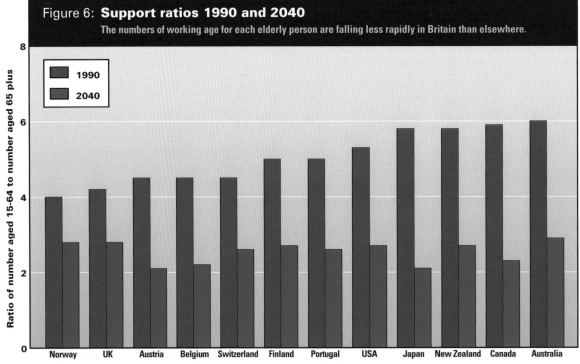

Figure 6: **Support ratios 1990 and 2040**

The numbers of working age for each elderly person are falling less rapidly in Britain than elsewhere.

Ratio of number aged 15-64 to number aged 65 plus

Legend: 1990, 2040

Countries (left to right): Norway, UK, Austria, Belgium, Switzerland, Finland, Portugal, USA, Japan, New Zealand, Canada, Australia

Source: OECD database. Forecasts are for 2031 (Australia and New Zealand), 2035 (Portugal) and 2036 (Canada).

To give a comparative picture, **Figure 6** shows how many people there were of working age (15-64) for each person of 65 or more in 1990 and forecasts for 2040 in various countries.[6] In 1990, this 'support ratio' was lower in Britain than anywhere else shown except Norway. But by 2040, the forecast is for the ratio to be *higher* in Britain than anywhere else except Australia (in 2031). Although Britain's support ratio is falling, it is doing so less quickly than in other countries. We already have an elderly population of significant size, and even by 2041, nearly three-quarters of the population is still forecast to be aged below 65. Importantly, not all welfare spending goes on the elderly population, so a 50 per cent rise in its population share only adds 17 per cent to average spending.

Other pressures

Another major pressure is the maturing of the State Earnings Related Pension Scheme (SERPS; see p 49). In 1994-95, SERPS payments cost under £2 billion. By 2040-41, the Government

Actuary (1995) forecast that costs would rise to £17-19.5 billion at 1994-95 prices, before allowing for the cuts in the 1995 Pension Act. Allowing for the higher incomes implied by these forecasts (more than doubling by then) the increase in the *gross* cost of SERPS over 50 years comes to over 1 per cent of GDP.[7] In addition, more people, especially married women, are becoming entitled to a full basic pension. However, as these payments rise, they reduce the need for Income Support for some and increase taxes for others. The *net* effect of SERPS over fifty years -which is what matters for public finances - would be smaller. Taking account of the effects of the pensions reforms, including the rise in married women's pension age, as forecast by the Government Actuary, together with the flow-back from higher taxes and effects on other benefits, these factors would add about 0.7 per cent of GDP to the effect of ageing by itself.

Other pressures include the rising number of lone parents and the rise in the cost of

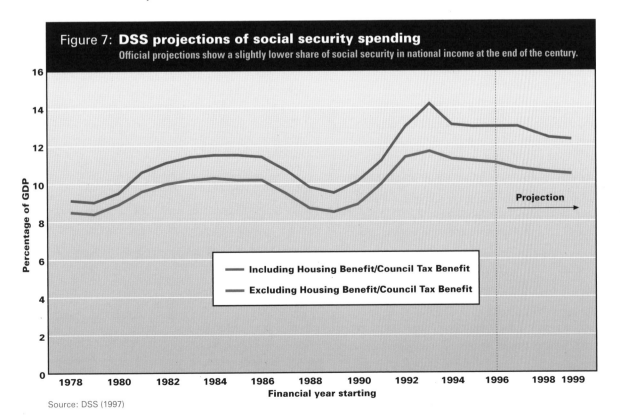

Figure 7: **DSS projections of social security spending**
Official projections show a slightly lower share of social security in national income at the end of the century.

Including Housing Benefit/Council Tax Benefit

Excluding Housing Benefit/Council Tax Benefit

Percentage of GDP

Financial year starting

Source: DSS (1997)

Incapacity Benefit as the larger numbers now receiving it at any given age carry on doing so when older.[8]

Figure 7 shows the Department of Social Security's (1997) projections of social security spending (including and excluding Housing Benefit and Council Tax Benefit)[9] to the turn of the century. The cost of social security is forecast to fall slowly as a share of GDP from its peak in 1993-94. Excluding Housing Benefit, its share of GDP in 1999-2000 is forecast to be just above the level it reached in the mid-1980s. The rising cost of Housing Benefit is discussed in Part 2.

Crisis, what *sort of* crisis?

So, over the medium term, Britain's welfare spending has been stable as a share of GDP; that share is below its equivalent in many other countries; and official projections do not show alarming growth in spending to the end of the century. There are upward pressures, notably from the ageing of the population, from SERPS and from higher basic pension entitlements. But, even if benefit levels were to keep up with overall living standards (which is not current policy), the net effects of these three factors on the public finances over the *fifty* years to 2040 would add up to less than 5 per cent of GDP - no more than the increase related to recession over the *three* years to 1992.

But this does not mean there are no problems. First, the share of welfare spending in GDP has been kept in check despite the large increase in unemployment since the 1970s through a series of measures which translate into 'cuts' in terms of level of provision for particular needs. Most importantly, social security benefits have, since the early 1980s, been linked to *prices* not to any measure of contemporary living standards. The DSS's projections in Figure 7 assume that this continues.

Second, even a stable share of welfare spending in national income is incompatible with aspirations for a falling share of tax in national income (unless borrowing rose, or other spending was cut).

Given that there will continue to be long-term upward pressures on welfare spending (although the rate of economic growth is probably the key factor) there are three options:

● Keeping the share of welfare down by continuing to let benefit levels fall behind contemporary living standards.
● Maintaining (or even improving) provision in relation both to need and contemporary living standards, accepting a slow (but by no means alarming) rise in the share of welfare spending in GDP, and hence in the taxes or contributions required to pay for it.
● Changing the structure of welfare provision so that the relative value of certain items was maintained, but others were cut out, so that the growth of the total was reduced or removed.

Further reading
Fewer Babies, Longer Lives, John Ermisch (JRF, 1990; see also Social Policy *Findings* No. 7).

The Growth of Social Security, Department of Social Security (HMSO, 1993).

'How will the scissors close? Options for UK social spending', John Hills (in *Britain Divided* edited by Alan Walker and Carol Walker, CPAG, 1997).

The State of Welfare: The welfare state in Britain since 1974, edited by John Hills (Oxford, 1990; second edition to be published in 1998).

Who benefits from welfare? Who pays?

In examining who benefits from the welfare state, it is important to be clear about who one would *expect* to be benefiting. Welfare services are often discussed as if their only purpose was the relief of poverty, but this was never their primary purpose. Much wider justifications have been advanced, some implying that benefits should go not only to the poorest.

There are at least five key aims - some overlapping - for public provision or finance of welfare services:[10]

(a) Relief of poverty and redistribution towards the long-term poor;

(b) Insurance of all against life's risks like long-term illness, unemployment, early retirement, family breakdown, and so on (where, for one reason or another, private insurance provision may not be very successful);

(c) Redistribution towards particular groups with greater needs - such as for medical care, disability, or family circumstances (such needs can be recognised for some by tax allowances as well as spending);

(d) Smoothing out the level of income over the life cycle, acting as a kind of 'savings bank' between periods of high earning and others of education or retirement;

(e) Stepping in where the 'family' fails - for instance, as a redistributive mechanism where women are left alone or with little by way of pension rights after divorce.

The redistributive effect of the welfare state cannot be judged just by looking at who *benefits*. You also have to look at who *pays* for it through the tax system. It is the *net* effect of benefits and the taxes which finance them which is crucial.

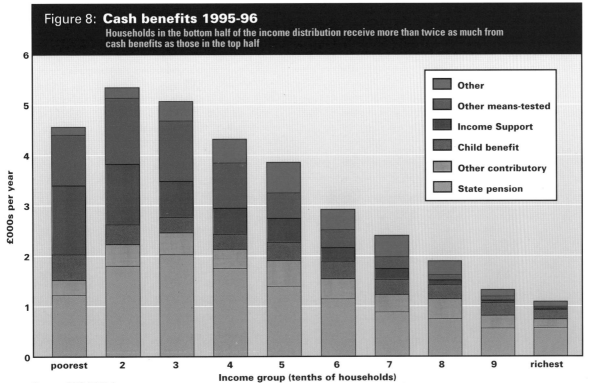

Figure 8: **Cash benefits 1995-96**

Households in the bottom half of the income distribution receive more than twice as much from cash benefits as those in the top half

Legend:
- Other
- Other means-tested
- Income Support
- Child benefit
- Other contributory
- State pension

Y-axis: £000s per year
X-axis: Income group (tenths of households) — poorest, 2, 3, 4, 5, 6, 7, 8, 9, richest

Source: ONS (1997a)
Note: Households are ranked by equivalent disposable income

15

(a) Redistribution in a single year

The present system already 'targets' those with lower incomes to a larger extent than often realised. **Figure 8** shows the average cash benefits received by different income groups in 1995-96. Households are arranged in order of 'disposable' income (that is, after receiving cash benefits and paying direct taxes like income tax), after allowing for the greater needs of bigger households (technically, by calculating 'equivalent' income).

On average, households in the bottom half of the distribution received 2.4 times as much as those in the top half. Means-tested benefits like Income Support are most concentrated on the poorest, but even 'universal' benefits like the state pension are worth more to lower than to higher income households.

Notably, the bottom tenth receives *less* on average than the next two groups. One of the reasons why households are in the bottom tenth is that, for one reason or another, they are not entitled to benefits, or fail to claim those which they could get.

Given that the absolute value of cash benefits is greatest for low-income households, and that their incomes from the market are low, benefits are of much greater *relative* importance at the bottom. Cash benefits represent 69 per cent of the gross income (including benefits) of the poorest tenth, but only 2 per cent for the richest tenth.

Figure 9 shows official estimates of the distribution between households of benefits 'in kind', such as from the National Health Service or state education. These suggest that benefits in kind are less concentrated on the poor than cash benefits, but households at the bottom of the distribution still receive more than those at the top (particularly from the NHS). Again, this pattern leads to a further reduction in income inequalities.

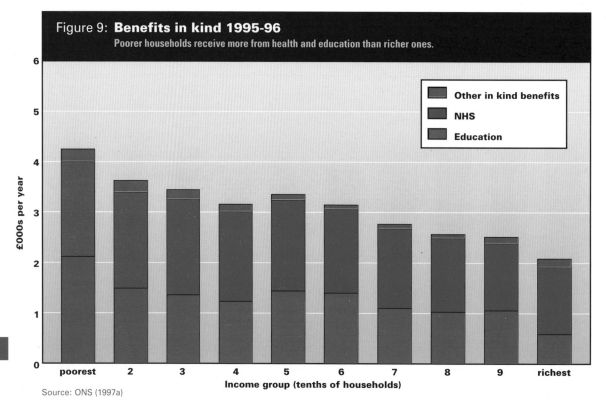

Figure 9: **Benefits in kind 1995-96**
Poorer households receive more from health and education than richer ones.

Legend:
- Other in kind benefits
- NHS
- Education

y-axis: £000s per year
x-axis: Income group (tenths of households) — poorest, 2, 3, 4, 5, 6, 7, 8, 9, richest

Source: ONS (1997a)

Other analyses (Evandrou *et al.*, 1993; Sefton, 1997) confirm these general findings using data from other sources. The estimates from these data allow for higher education spending on students away from home, suggesting that, if anything, benefits from education spending are less concentrated on the poor. On the other hand, they suggest that housing subsidies - heavily concentrated on the poor - are greater in scale than the official estimates. Overall, people on middle incomes received rather more from benefits in kind then shown in Figure 9, but these analyses confirmed that their value was lowest for those at the top of the income scale.

By contrast to benefits, taxation represents much the same *proportion* of gross income for rich and poor alike.[11] Direct taxes take an increasing percentage share as gross incomes rise, but the reverse is true of indirect taxes (like excise duties and VAT). The net effects of welfare benefits and all taxes (some of which finance non-welfare items)[12] can be seen

comparing the 'original' incomes (ie before taxes and benefits) with 'final' incomes (after taxes and benefits) in **Figure 10**. Although those with higher incomes do benefit from the welfare state and despite the largely proportional (rather than progressive) tax system, the bottom five income groups are gainers from the combination, the top five losers.

Even 'universal' benefits and services are redistributive towards those with lower incomes if the absolute size of the tax payments which finance them rises with income or if the contingencies covered affect the poor more than the rich. As a corollary, reducing such benefits in order to keep down taxes is in the interests of the rich, not of the poor.

(b) Life cycle redistribution
Redistribution between rich and poor is only one of the aims advanced for the welfare state. Much of what the welfare state does is actually

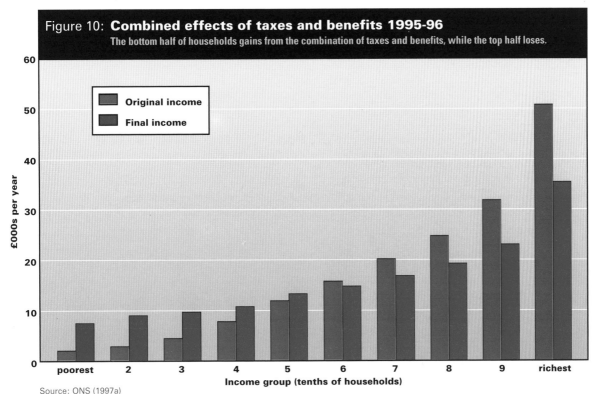

Figure 10: **Combined effects of taxes and benefits 1995-96**
The bottom half of households gains from the combination of taxes and benefits, while the top half loses.

Source: ONS (1997a)
Note: Original income is before taxes and benefits. Final income is after direct and indirect taxes and includes benefits in cash and kind.

to redistribute across the *life cycle*, between times of relative 'want' and relative 'plenty'.

Measuring life-cycle effects of benefits and taxes is not straightforward. No surveys yet cover individuals for their whole lives, and even if they existed, they would tell us about the effects of a series of systems, rather than isolating those of today's system. The findings presented below are therefore drawn from a computer model of 4,000 individual life histories, LIFEMOD.[13] The simulated life histories in the model are very varied - reflecting the great diversity of incomes and family histories found in the British population in the mid-1980s (with income levels adjusted here to those of 1991). The model is very detailed, allowing us to build up the effects of the tax and welfare systems on the assumption that the systems remain in a 'steady state' for the model individuals' complete lives.[14]

Figure 11 shows how average incomes move with age for individuals in the model. The

'equivalent' incomes shown allow for family circumstances and assume (in the results shown here) equal sharing between couples.

● **'Original'** incomes (before taxes and benefits are taken into account) rise steeply at first, flatten out, then reach a peak in late middle age (the 'empty nest'), before dropping sharply in retirement.
● Cash benefits and direct taxes reduce incomes before retirement but boost it thereafter. As a result, **net** incomes follow a much flatter pattern.
● Allowing further for benefits in kind from education and health gives **final** income.[15] The importance of the health service for those over 65 is clear (although this is a response to their needs, rather than a boost to their living standards).

The figure shows how the combination of the welfare benefits and direct taxes - as they were structured and with their relative generosity in 1991 - succeeds in smoothing out a considerable

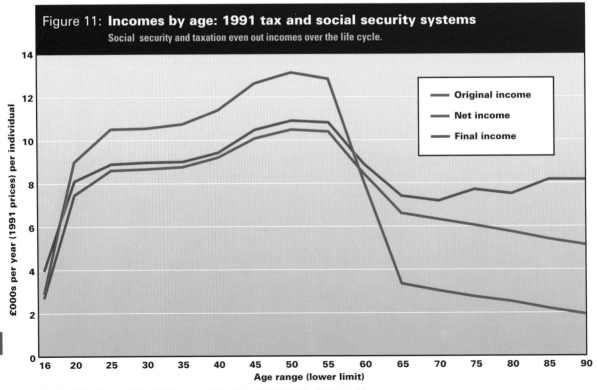

Figure 11: **Incomes by age: 1991 tax and social security systems**

Source: Falkingham and Hills (1995); results derived from LIFEMOD simulation model.
Note: Incomes are equivalent incomes assuming equal sharing between couples and using the McClements equivalence scale. Net income is after direct tax and cash benefits. Final income includes education and health benefits.

amount of the variation in living standards over the life cycle. People 'pay into' the system at times in their lives when incomes are relatively high, but 'draw out' from it when they are relatively low.

(c) Redistribution between lifetime rich and lifetime poor

It could be that the *only* effect of the welfare state is to redistribute income across individuals' life cycles - the 'savings bank' effect. Even if the poor in any given year benefit from the welfare state while the rich pay for it, there might still be no redistribution at all between different people, when everything is totalled over complete lifetimes.

Figure 12 presents results from LIFEMOD bearing on this. The bars show the position of individuals over their complete lives, arranged in income groups reflecting their average *lifetime* living standards, with the 'lifetime poorest' on the left. The top panel shows total lifetime benefits from social security, education and the NHS going to each income group. The 'lifetime poorest' receive somewhat more than the 'lifetime richest', but the overall distribution of gross benefits is very flat: almost regardless of income, someone could expect to receive gross benefits over their life totalling around £133,000 (at 1991 prices).

Over their lives, people both receive benefits and pay taxes. Those with higher lifetime incomes pay much more tax than those with low incomes. In effect, people finance some of the benefits they receive through their own lifetime tax payments. However, some people do not pay enough lifetime tax to pay for all of the benefits they receive; they receive net lifetime benefits from the system. These net lifetime benefits are paid for by others who pay more than enough tax to finance their own benefits; they pay net lifetime taxes into the system.

The bars in the top panel of Figure 12 are therefore divided into two. The bottom part shows the proportion of benefits which is 'self-financed' and this rises for higher lifetime income groups. The bars in the lower panel show where the net lifetime taxes are coming from.[16] Net lifetime taxes also rise moving up through the income groups.

Finally, the line in the lower panel shows the net gain or loss from the system to each lifetime income group as a whole. The bottom five groups are net gainers on average; the sixth group breaks even; the top four groups are net losers.

The system does therefore redistribute quite successfully from 'lifetime rich' to 'lifetime poor'. However, the diagram suggests that *most* benefits are self-financed over people's lifetimes, rather than being paid for by others. Of the £133,000 average gross lifetime benefits from the system, an average of £98,000 is self-financed. Nearly three-quarters of what the welfare state does looked at in this way is like a 'savings bank'; only a quarter is 'Robin Hood' redistribution between different people.[17]

The policy implications are important. Scaling down the public welfare system would either hit ordinary people at times in their lives when their incomes were lowest or would mean they would have to pay more in good times for private means of smoothing income. There is a legitimate debate over whether income smoothing is best done publicly or privately, but either way the cost cannot be escaped.

(d) Redistribution between generations

The welfare state may mainly be a kind of savings bank, but the bank does not actually have any money in it. Instead, it is financed on a 'Pay as You Go' (PAYG) basis. There is an implicit contract under which each working

19

generation aged from 20 to 59 pays more into the system than it receives from it, covering education for the young and health care and

pensions for the elderly. At 1991 values, those aged 59 would on average have paid cumulatively over £40,000 more into the system

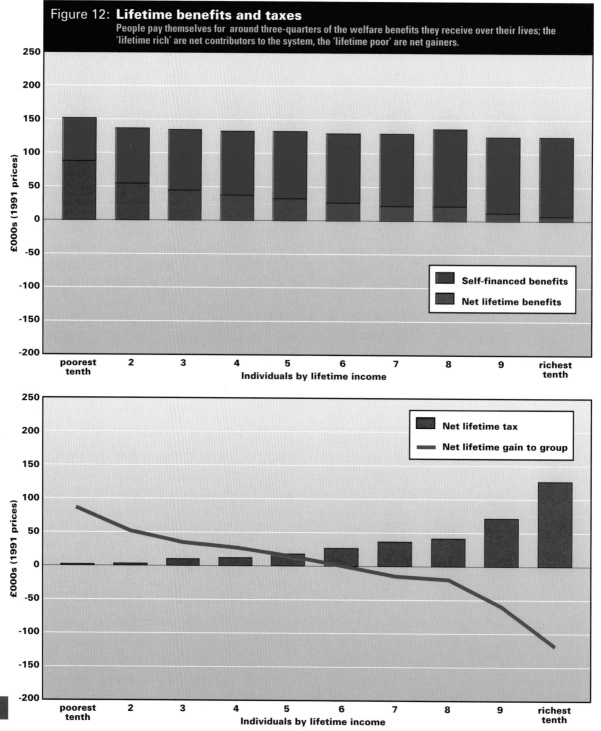

Figure 12: **Lifetime benefits and taxes**

People pay themselves for around three-quarters of the welfare benefits they receive over their lives; the 'lifetime rich' are net contributors to the system, the 'lifetime poor' are net gainers.

Source: Falkingham and Hills (1995). Results derived from LIFEMOD simulation model.
Notes: 1 Individuals are ranked by lifetime equivalent net incomes.
       2 Calculations allow for share of tax bills necessary to pay for cost of welfare benefits (23% of gross incomes).
       3 Results use structure and relative generosity of 1991 tax and benefit systems.

than they had received; they would expect to receive all of this back over the rest of their lives.

Analysis suggests that, despite the great increase in the scale of the welfare state between the end of the War and the mid-1970s, most 'generations' (five-year age cohorts) will get nearly as much out of the system as they put into it (some slightly more), *provided* that something roughly equivalent to the current system continues.[18] However, if the size of the welfare state is scaled back as a share of GDP, those age groups currently aged about 35-64 end up getting rather less out of the system than they put in. They would have 'paid in' to the savings bank, but would only get back part of what they paid in.

(e) Redistribution between men and women

The welfare state also redistributes from men to women. Men have higher earnings and pay more tax than women. Women live longer than men and receive more from the welfare state because of this and because of their lower original incomes. Looking at the LIFEMOD results for men and women separately, women receive a net average lifetime gain from the welfare state of just over £50,000 (at 1991 prices) and men make an average lifetime contribution of the same amount.

An important function of the welfare state is thus partially to reduce the imbalance in lifetime living standards between men and women. A corollary is that decreases in the relative generosity of the welfare state benefit men but imply losses for women (taking each sex as a whole).

Summary: The welfare state and distribution

The welfare state does much more than redistribute between rich and poor in a single year, although it clearly does this relatively successfully once one takes into account the taxes which pay for it. It smoothes out income over the life cycle, acting as a kind of 'savings bank'. That may, in fact, be most of what it does, but it also redistributes from the 'lifetime rich' to the 'lifetime poor'. On average, women are net lifetime beneficiaries from the system, men net lifetime payers for it.

The scale of and balance between these different results are key political questions. What is clear is that there are many more dimensions of the welfare state's effects to take into account when considering its future than just narrow questions about the income levels of the direct beneficiaries from any one part of it.

Further reading

'The effects of taxes and benefits on household income, 1995-96', Office of National Statistics (*Economic Trends*, March 1997)

'Welfare benefits in kind and income distribution', Maria Evandrou, Jane Falkingham, John Hills and Julian Le Grand (*Fiscal Studies*, February, 1993)

The Changing Distribution of the Social Wage, Tom Sefton (STICERD Occasional Paper 21, London School of Economics, 1997)

The Dynamic of Welfare: Social policy and the life cycle, edited by Jane Falkingham and John Hills (Harvester Wheatsheaf, 1995)

Side-effects of welfare provision

People have probably worried about the 'incentive' effects of welfare provision since the Prodigal Son returned - would others now live riotously, secure in the promise of fatted calves when their money ran out?

Today a small industry of economists is trying to identify how welfare provision affects people's decisions to stay on in education; to work; how many hours to work; to remain unemployed; to have children; to marry or be a lone parent; to register as sick; to visit the doctor; to save; or to retire. Firm conclusions from this work are, however, rare and seemingly clear results are often quickly clouded by further studies reaching different conclusions.[19]

This lack of decisive conclusions reflects the complexity of human life in general and of the welfare state in particular. Decisions on the

kind of life choices listed above depend on far more than narrow monetary considerations. Just because an incentive exists, does not mean that people necessarily act on it. Even when money is important, individual circumstances vary enormously. One can construct particular examples with overwhelming pressures in one direction, but these can be atypical or ignore how welfare provision actually operates - for instance, disqualification or reductions in benefit for the 'voluntarily unemployed'.

Incomes in and out of work

Figure 13 gives an example of the 'unemployment trap' - where people can be 'better off on the dole' than in work. For someone entitled to full assistance with mortgage interest, earnings of about £100 per week would be needed for net income in work to exceed that on Income Support (means-tested

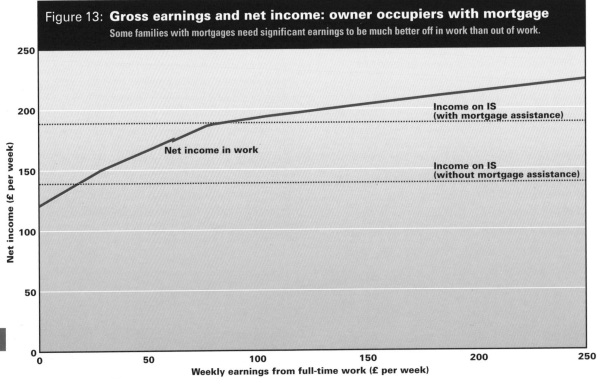

Figure 13: **Gross earnings and net income: owner occupiers with mortgage**
Some families with mortgages need significant earnings to be much better off in work than out of work.

Income on IS (with mortgage assistance)

Net income in work

Income on IS (without mortgage assistance)

Net income (£ per week)

Weekly earnings from full-time work (£ per week)

Source: own calculations
Note: couple; children aged 6 and 13; one full time earner; Council Tax £9.21/week; £40,000 mortgage (interest of £44.38 per week); 1997-98

Job Seekers Allowance). While some of the features are general, a particular factor in this case is the mortgage assistance: for a tenant with a low rent, or someone with a recent mortgage not entitled to help when on Income Support, there would be a net gain from work at much lower earnings levels.

However, such extreme examples are not, in fact, typical. **Figure 14** draws on results from a DSS survey of men and women who became unemployed in 1987. It shows their net incomes out of work as a percentage of their previous net incomes in work. For 53 per cent of the sample, out of work incomes were less than half those in work; only for one in six of the sample (but a quarter of the women) was this 'replacement rate' (out of work income as a percentage of income in work) more than 80 per cent. Since 1987, benefit changes have reduced replacement rates further. By 1996-97 official estimates were that only 5.3 per cent of the whole working population faced replacement rates above 70 per cent.[20]

The 'poverty trap'
Figure 15 shows another well-known phenomenon, the 'poverty trap'. In this example, someone with earnings of £160 per week would end up only £13.50 better off than someone with earnings of £60 per week. It is as if they had to pay tax of 86 per cent on their extra earnings - more than twice the current maximum rate for people with the highest incomes. This happens because the extra income is not only taxed, but its receipt also reduces entitlement to means-tested benefits like Housing Benefit and Family Credit.

This phenomenon is an inevitable corollary of greater 'targeting' of benefits through reliance on means-testing - for instance, the switch from 'bricks and mortar' housing subsidies to Housing Benefit (see Figures 47 and 48). **Figure 16** shows official estimates of the number of family units where at least one partner worked 'full-time' (in benefit terms) facing 'marginal tax rates' of this kind exceeding 50 per cent. In 1996-97 just over 700,000 did so.

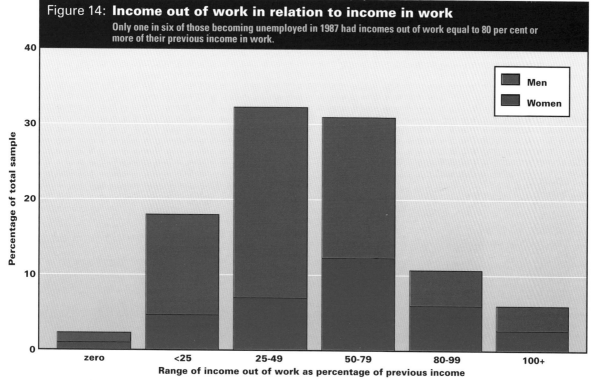

Figure 14: **Income out of work in relation to income in work**

Only one in six of those becoming unemployed in 1987 had incomes out of work equal to 80 per cent or more of their previous income in work.

Source: Garman et al (1992), Table 3.24

23

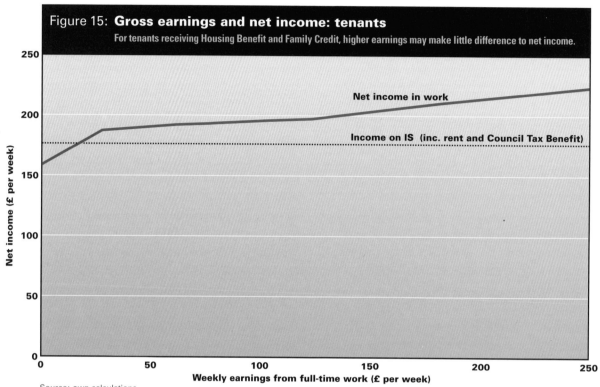

Figure 15: Gross earnings and net income: tenants

For tenants receiving Housing Benefit and Family Credit, higher earnings may make little difference to net income.

Net income in work

Income on IS (inc. rent and Council Tax Benefit)

Net income (£ per week)

Weekly earnings from full-time work (£ per week)

Source: own calculations
Note: couple; children aged 6 and 13; one full time earner; Council Tax £9.21/week; rent £37.62/week; 1997-98

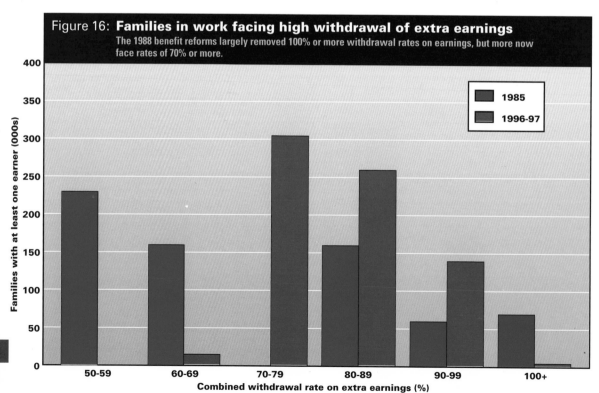

Figure 16: Families in work facing high withdrawal of extra earnings

The 1988 benefit reforms largely removed 100% or more withdrawal rates on earnings, but more now face rates of 70% or more.

1985

1996-97

Families with at least one earner (000s)

Combined withdrawal rate on extra earnings (%)

Source: DSS (1997), Figure 34

24

Figure 16 compares the situation in 1985, before the 'Fowler' reforms implemented in 1988, with that in 1996-97. The reforms largely removed the problem of people losing *more than* 100 per cent of any extra income, ending up worse off though earning more. However, more than twice as many people face rates above 70 per cent (only partly reflecting changed definitions of full-time work).

These figures are for families *in work*. Those out of work and receiving Income Support lose 100 per cent of any additional part-time earnings after the first £5 until they lose entitlement to it altogether. In 1995-96, 1.9 million unemployed non-pensioners were receiving Income Support and in this position (excluding single parents, whose position is discussed below).[21]

Partners of the unemployed

Much of the incentive debate focuses on the first earner in a couple, usually the man. But one of the firmer conclusions of incentive researchers is that the labour supply of married

women is sensitive to income differences.[22] Here the precise form of the benefit system can be very important.

Figure 17 shows the net income of a childless couple where the husband is unemployed, but his wife has a part-time job earning £100 net per week. In the first case, she carries on working but he is not entitled to non-means-tested Job Seekers Allowance (JSA), and they claim Housing Benefit and Council Tax Benefit. They are only £3.40 per week better off than in the second case, where neither works and they claim means-tested JSA. In the third case, however, he is entitled to non-means-tested JSA. If she earns £100 net per week, they are £25 per week better off than if neither works.

If tightening up on qualification conditions for non-means-tested unemployment benefits[23] has pushed couples from position 3 to position 1, not only are they worse off, but they may also decide the return on her work is too low, and end up in

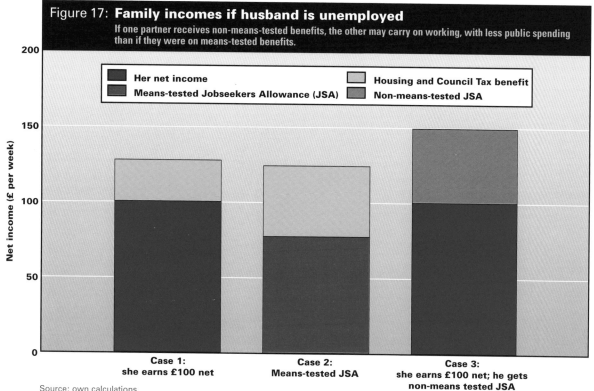

Figure 17: Family incomes if husband is unemployed

If one partner receives non-means-tested benefits, the other may carry on working, with less public spending than if they were on means-tested benefits.

Legend:
- Her net income
- Means-tested Jobseekers Allowance (JSA)
- Housing and Council Tax benefit
- Non-means-tested JSA

Y-axis: Net income (£ per week), 0 to 200

Case 1: she earns £100 net
Case 2: Means-tested JSA
Case 3: she earns £100 net; he gets non-means tested JSA

Source: own calculations
Note: Tenant couple paying rent of £37.62 and Council Tax of £9.21 per week; 1997-98

position 2 - resulting in much *higher* public spending than in Case 3. The net return from the husband taking a new job is also smaller if she is not working, which may increase his length of time out of work and claiming benefit.

The low net returns from work for the wives of unemployed men have been blamed for what is shown in **Figure 18**. Increasingly, couples of working age are tending to polarise between two-earner and no-earner couples. Only 33 per cent of the wives of unemployed or economically inactive men were in employment in 1991, compared to 74 per cent of those with employed husbands.[24] However, research discourages a purely economistic explanation of this: other factors, such as class differences, the presence of pre-school children and age may be as important.[25]

Becoming a lone parent
A major theme in Charles Murray's (1984) assault on the US welfare system was the proposition that benefits have encouraged women to become lone parents and hence induced 'dependency'. He focused on Aid to Families with Dependent Children (AFDC) for which, unlike equivalent British benefits, couples may not be eligible. Murray's analysis has since been hotly disputed.[26] In Britain concern has been expressed that teenage girls deliberately become pregnant to 'jump the housing queue' as lone parents.

Bradshaw and Millar (1991) found, like previous research, little evidence for young women deliberately becoming pregnant to gain such advantages: for 92 per cent of single parents who had their first child as teenagers, the pregnancy was unplanned. Only 1 per cent of all lone parents cited financial benefits as a reason for separation or not living together.

Lone parents and work incentives
Lone parents on Income Support can earn £15 per week before benefit is lost pound for pound with higher earnings. Since April 1992, those

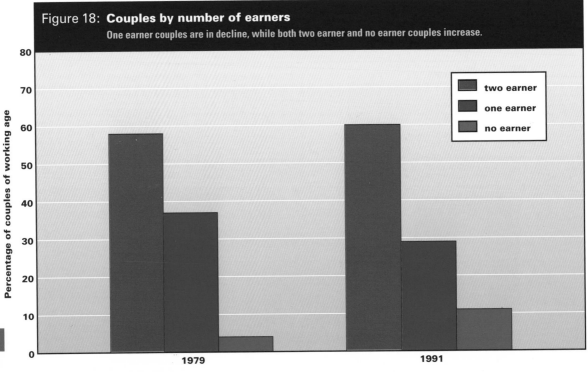

Figure 18: **Couples by number of earners**
One earner couples are in decline, while both two earner and no earner couples increase.

Source: OPCS (1981), Table 5.8 and OPCS (1993a), Table 5.27
Note: 1979 figures are for married couples where both are of working age. 1991 figures are for
married couples where husband is aged 16-64.

working more than 16 hours a week qualify for Family Credit in place of Income Support. Some childcare costs can now be taken into account ('disregarded') in calculating Family Credit. The shape of the poverty and unemployment traps facing lone parents differs from those affecting two-parent families. Because most lone parents are women, typically with lower wages than men, only a minority are likely to find jobs which pay enough to get clear of the poverty trap.

Figure 19 shows the net income after housing costs of a lone parent with two young children depending on her hours of work at a rate of £3.50 per hour. With no maintenance or child-care costs, she could find herself on one of three 'poverty plateaux', with no change in income between 5 and 15 hours per week, then a jump, and then only slow increases between 16 and 30 hours a week and again after 30 hours (until Family Credit ends).

If she receives £40 per week maintenance (£15 of which is 'disregarded' in calculating Family Credit, but not Income Support), the jump at 16 hours per week is greater, and, theoretically, her net income would accelerate earlier, after working 40 hours per week. On the other hand, if she receives no maintenance but has to pay £1.50 per hour for a child-minder, she is no better off working 50 hours than working 20 hours, and worse off working 10 to 14 hours than not working at all.

A 1991 survey found that lone parents were on average about £30 per week better off in work and claiming Family Credit than out of work on Income Support. However, once on Family Credit they typically only kept 20 pence out of each extra £1 of earnings.[27]

Not surprisingly, lone parents have different employment patterns from other parents. Only 43 per cent were employed in 1989-91, compared to 62 per cent for married women with children. The key difference is in the

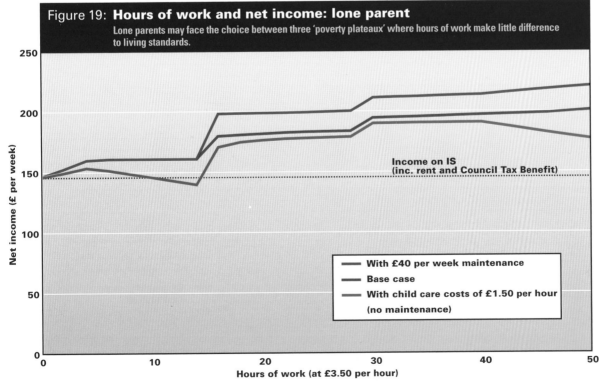

Figure 19: **Hours of work and net income: lone parent**
Lone parents may face the choice between three 'poverty plateaux' where hours of work make little difference to living standards.

Source: own calculations
Note: single parent; children aged 3 and 6; Council Tax £9.21/week; rent £37.62/week; 1997-98

proportion working part-time: only 14 per cent of those with a child under 5 and 32 per cent with older children. These compare with 32 and 47 per cent for equivalent married mothers.[28] Employment rates are also lower than the EU average, where 54 per cent of lone parents are in employment, and 38 per cent working full-time (18 per cent in the UK).[29] As well as benefit structure, a key causal factor may be that Britain has fewer places in publicly funded day care than nearly all European countries.[30]

Positive labour market effects

Even in theory, not all of the effects of welfare on the labour market are necessarily negative.[31] Positive effects include:

● The existence of some kind of 'social safety net' for those losing their jobs reduces the risks to workers of jobs in innovative new businesses, which may be important for the economy but carry a risk of failure.

● Similarly, without a social security system, economic restructuring would be far more difficult, as people would have much stronger incentives to hang on to jobs in declining industries.

● Firms offering permanent employment take on greater risks than those offering insecure work. State unemployment insurance - the conditions for which are more often met for permanent workers - reduces the risks to workers in such firms. In effect, it may act as a kind of subsidy to firms offering 'good jobs'.

● The structure of maternity benefits and maternity leave play a major role in encouraging women to return to employment. Those women who return after taking maternity leave have much higher earnings in their early thirties than those who have children, but change jobs.[32]

Looking beyond social security, the 'social' returns from time spent in education or training are greater than those accruing just to the student or trainee. State provision or finance can bring individual and social returns closer together and lead to better decisions for the

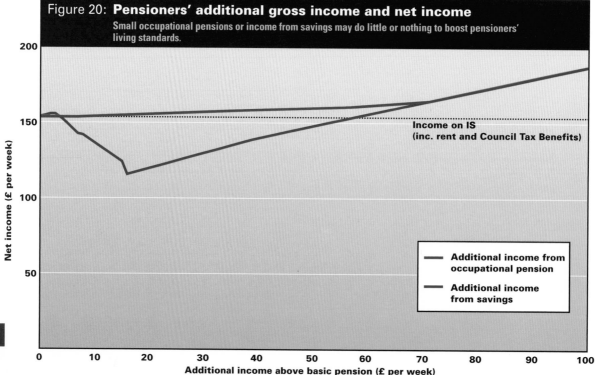

Figure 20: **Pensioners' additional gross income and net income**

Small occupational pensions or income from savings may do little or nothing to boost pensioners' living standards.

Income on IS
(inc. rent and Council Tax Benefits)

Additional income from occupational pension

Additional income from savings

Net income (£ per week)

Additional income above basic pension (£ per week)

Source: own calculations
Note: pensioner couple receiving basic pension; rent £37.62/week; Council Tax £9.21/week; 1997-98

whole economy.[33] Similarly, the provision of health care for workers improves the productivity of the workforce. Beveridge himself described the health service as "rehabilitation services for prevention and cure of disease and restoration of capacity for work".[34]

Saving for retirement

There is a major economic debate as to whether the existence of 'pay as you go' universal state pensions (ie tax-financed, rather than paid from accumulated funds) lead people to work and save less than otherwise for additional income in retirement. While this debate is unresolved,[35] a much sharper incentive problem, analogous to the 'unemployment trap', can result from the operation of means-tested benefits for retired people with small incomes from savings or occupational pensions.

Figure 20 shows how total net income varies with private income for a tenant couple entitled to the full basic married pension. There is no gain at all from having an occupational pension of less than £7 per week, and little gain until it is over £72. It is actually a disadvantage to have savings generating investment income of between £5 and £55 per week.[36]

If people realise that they will face this position in advance, they may decide there is little point in saving or building up pension rights below a threshold. If they do not realise it in advance, they are likely to turn round afterwards and ask why they bothered to put money aside. Neither outcome is satisfactory. Policies which widen the gap between the basic pension and Income Support rates widen the income range affected. The phenomenon is particularly acute for those requiring residential care and receiving means-tested support via their local authorities.

Conclusion

The verdict on whether unfavourable side-effects do result from welfare provision may in many cases be 'not proven'. But this does not remove the need to worry about potential problems. First, even if it is hard to discern individual responses to their own circumstances, the belief that, for instance, 'people are better off on the dole' may affect people's behaviour, even if in their own case it is untrue. Second, the key element of behaviour affected may be declaration of income to the DSS or tax office, rather than economic activity itself.

Finally, perverse incentives may also be seen as *inequitable*. The Prodigal Son's brother saw it as *unfair* that a fatted calf was slain for his brother but never for him, despite many years of work. Not only is inequity a problem in itself, but it may bring the whole system into disrepute and threaten its future.

Further reading

The Economics of the Welfare State, Nicholas Barr (Weidenfeld and Nicholson, new edition 1993)

'Income maintenance and social insurance: a survey', A. B. Atkinson, in *Handbook of Public Economics*, edited by A. Auerbach and M. Feldstein (Elsevier, 1987)

'Economic theory and the welfare state: A survey and reinterpretation', Nicholas Barr (*Journal of Economic Literature*, June 1992)

Families, Work and Benefits, Alan Marsh and Stephen McKay (PSI, 1993)

Lone Parents, Work and Benefits, Alan Marsh, Reuben Ford and Louise Finlayson (DSS, 1997)

Private lives and public responses: lone parenthood and future policy, Reuben Ford and Jane Millar (JRF Foundations, 1997)

Social and economic change

As well as questions about its future cost and current effectiveness, equally important to the future of the welfare state is the way in which the social environment is changing. These changes may leave parts of its structure already outmoded.

While parts have been added to it, and while Beveridge would see many departures from his intended model, much of today's social security system has its foundations in the recommend-ations of his famous wartime report on *Social Insurance and Allied Services* (1942). Those recommendations were themselves founded on a series of assumptions about social and economic structures, many of which have since changed profoundly, raising the question whether social security - and perhaps education and health policies which have similar 1940s foundations - requires reform to meet fifty years of social change.

Amongst the circumstances or assumptions underlying Beveridge's proposals were:

(a) A population in which fewer than 10 per cent were aged 65 or more.
(b) While desertion or legal separation were an "economic risk" of marriage for women, widowhood was the main contingency on which to focus, and children would be born to and looked after by two legally married parents.
(c) Government would be committed to an active policy to maintain high employment (taken as meaning under 8.5 per cent unemployment, with unemployment over 6 months "a rare thing").[37] In peacetime, seven out of eight women would "follow no gainful occupation". Meanwhile, men of working age would fall largely into two categories, full-time employees and the unemployed or otherwise inactive, with few in any 'grey' areas between.

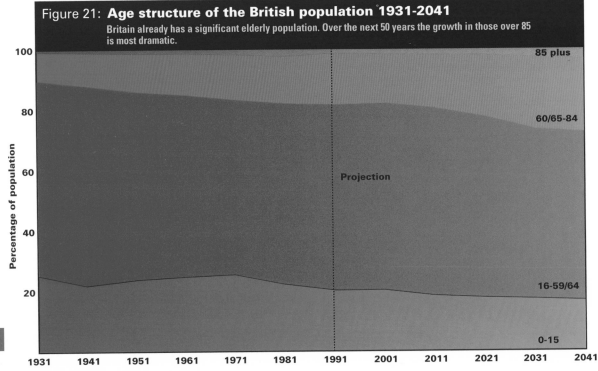

Figure 21: **Age structure of the British population 1931-2041**
Britain already has a significant elderly population. Over the next 50 years the growth in those over 85 is most dramatic.

Source: ONS (1996) and Mitchell (1988)

(d) The main causes of poverty (based on Rowntree's findings in 1936) could be dealt with through the proposed national insurance system, with few requiring a means-tested top up from what was established as National Assistance.

In effect the model was one of stable families with full-time male breadwinners, with income shortfalls resulting from a small number of identifiable causes. But, in each of the respects listed above, British society looks very different today. In addition, the distribution of incomes from the market has become steadily more unequal since the late 1970s, adding to the scale of the problems faced by the welfare state.

(a) The ageing population

Figure 21 shows the shares of key age groups in the British population since 1931, together with official projections for the next fifty years. By 1991, those over statutory pension age (60 for women, 65 for men) made up 18.5 per cent of

the population, compared with 11.4 per cent fifty years before, with further increases forecast (but note that the growth in the elderly population is partly offset by the fall in numbers under 16).

(b) Changing family structures[38]

By 1989, four per cent of adults were cohabiting but not married. Increasingly cohabiting before marriage is seen as the norm - two-thirds of those aged under 45 would advise a couple to do so. Between 1970 and 1991 the proportion of births in England and Wales occurring outside marriage rose from 8 to 30 per cent (but seven out of ten of such births are registered by two parents living at the same address). Between 1951 and 1987 the annual divorce rate rose from 2.6 to 12.7 per thousand married couples. If current divorce rates continue, 40 per cent of marriages will end in divorce and more than one in five children will experience a parental divorce by age 16.

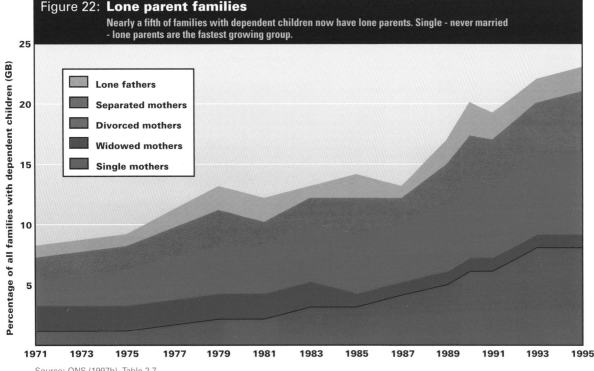

Figure 22: **Lone parent families**
Nearly a fifth of families with dependent children now have lone parents. Single - never married - lone parents are the fastest growing group.

Percentage of all families with dependent children (GB)

Lone fathers
Separated mothers
Divorced mothers
Widowed mothers
Single mothers

1971 1973 1975 1977 1979 1981 1983 1985 1987 1989 1991 1993 1995

Source: ONS (1997b), Table 2.7

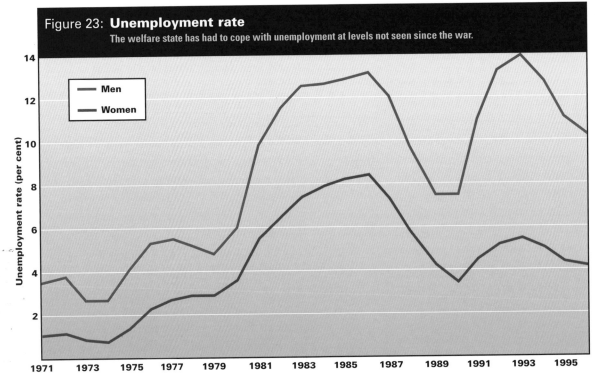

Figure 23: **Unemployment rate**

The welfare state has had to cope with unemployment at levels not seen since the war.

Source: Department of Employment
Note: Annual averages

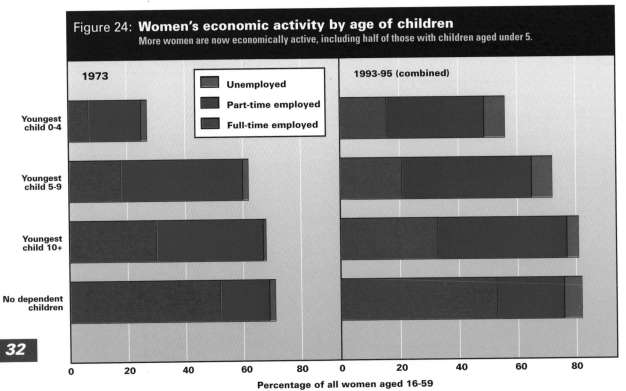

Figure 24: **Women's economic activity by age of children**

More women are now economically active, including half of those with children aged under 5.

Percentage of all women aged 16-59

Source: ONS (1997b), Table 4.11

As a result of these and other trends, the number of lone-parent families continues to increase, as shown in **Figure 22**, rising from 8 to 23 per cent of families with children between 1971 and 1995. Single (never-married) women are the most rapidly growing group of lone parents, and represent about one-third of the total.

At (mostly) the other end of the age range, 16 per cent of all adults in 1990 were caring informally in some way for someone who was sick, elderly, or disabled; for 4 per cent of adults, this was for someone within the home (Evandrou, 1993).

These changing family patterns have important implications for income distribution and social security:
● In 1989, 40 per cent of cohabiting couples with children had gross incomes below £200 per week - twice the proportion for married couples with children.
● In 1993/94, lone parents or their children - 8 per cent of the whole population - were 20 per

cent of the poorest fifth of all individuals.[39]
● In 1991, 79 per cent of lone mothers aged over 20 were receiving Income Support.
● In 1985, those caring for someone within their home had a median equivalent income 26 per cent below that of non-carers.[40]

(c) The labour market

Figure 23 shows the percentage of the labour force unemployed and claiming benefit since 1971 (the earliest date for consistent figures). This has, for men, been above the 8.5 per cent maximum level assumed by Beveridge for most of the period since 1981. In addition, the proportion of the unemployed who had been so for over a year in April 1997 was 39 per cent for men and 28 per cent for women. In all, over 600,000 people had been out of work for over a year.

At the same time, **Figure 24** shows how women's participation in the labour force has risen over the last two decades, particularly part-time work. Labour force participation by

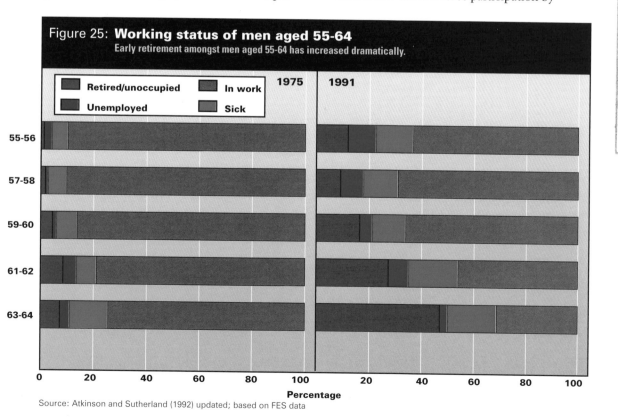

Figure 25: **Working status of men aged 55-64**
Early retirement amongst men aged 55-64 has increased dramatically.

Source: Atkinson and Sutherland (1992) updated; based on FES data

mothers with a child under five rose from 27 per cent in 1973 to 56 per cent in the years 1993-95 (combined), although participation rates still rise with the age of the youngest child.

The Beveridge Report was based on a total for "other gainfully employed" of 2.6 million, 11 per cent of the labour force. In the event, only about 1.7 million people were self-employed between 1951 and 1965. Since then self-employment has risen, reaching 1.9 million in 1979, and jumping to 3.4 million by 1990, over 12 per cent of the labour force (Brown, 1992).

These 'non-standard' forms of employment - like part-time work and self-employment - create problems for a system of social security which has its origins in a labour market dominated by full-time male employee breadwinners. Further problems result from early retirement which, in one form or another, has grown rapidly since the mid-1970s, as shown in **Figure 25**. By 1991, fewer than

half of men aged 61 or more were in work, compared to over three-quarters in the mid-1970s.

(d) Causes of poverty

Beveridge's proposals were heavily influenced by Rowntree's poverty surveys. Beveridge suggested that this showed causes directly amenable to social insurance - like unemployment and old age - accounted for five-sixths of primary poverty in 1936 (**Figure 26**). Hence national insurance - if rates were set high enough - could keep people out of poverty without recourse to a means test. The causes of poverty or low incomes have varied greatly since the War.

Figure 26 shows the latest comparable figures. In 1993/94 old age accounted for 23 per cent of those in the poorest fifth of the population, down from 39 per cent in 1979, while that related to unemployment was up to 23 from 10 per cent. By contrast with the pre-War figures,

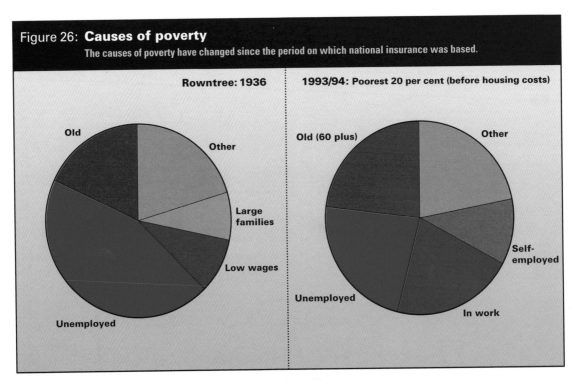

Figure 26: **Causes of poverty**
The causes of poverty have changed since the period on which national insurance was based.

Rowntree: 1936

1993/94: Poorest 20 per cent (before housing costs)

Source: Evans and Glennerster (1993) Figure 1 and DSS (1996a), Table D2 (BHC)

low incomes for people in work accounted for 21 per cent of the poorest in 1993/94 (although this was down from 30 per cent in 1979).

By 1990 only 30 per cent of the poorest tenth were recipients of national insurance benefits (Webb, 1994). In one sense, this is a *success* of the benefits in carrying recipients off the bottom of the distribution, where they would otherwise be - the greatest concentration of recipients was in the second poorest tenth (where 45 per cent receive them). But, for one reason or another, insurance benefits miss many of the poorest.

The growth of poverty and inequality

In addition to these general social and economic changes over the last fifty years, affecting the *kinds* of problems faced by the welfare state, there have been particularly rapid changes in the last few years in the *scale* of problems it faces with respect to those with low incomes. Britain has no official 'poverty line', nor any

official count of the numbers 'in poverty'. There are, however, two series of statistics which show trends in the numbers with low incomes defined in different ways, whether or not labelled as 'in poverty'.[41]

The first, the 'Low Income Families' series is illustrated in **Figure 27**. This counts the number of people with incomes at or below the levels which Income Support (formerly Supplementary Benefit) is intended to guarantee. In 1979, over four million people were in families living on Supplementary Benefit, and over three million fell below the State's safety net. Thirteen years later, the numbers living on the safety net had doubled, the numbers living below it had grown by a half.

These numbers depend on the relative generosity or otherwise of the safety net. Those taking an 'absolute' view (that poverty should be measured against a fixed standard, irrespective of living standards elsewhere in

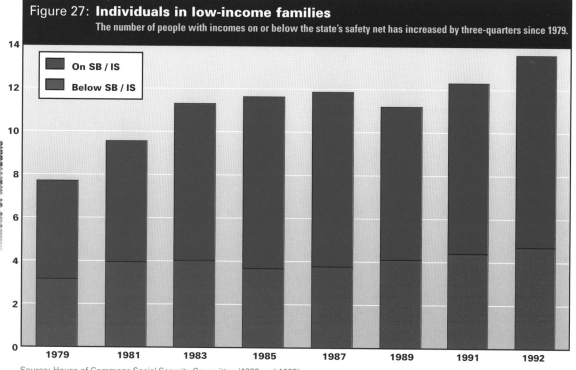

Figure 27: **Individuals in low-income families**
The number of people with incomes on or below the state's safety net has increased by three-quarters since 1979.

- On SB / IS
- Below SB / IS

Source: House of Commons Social Security Committee (1992 and 1995)

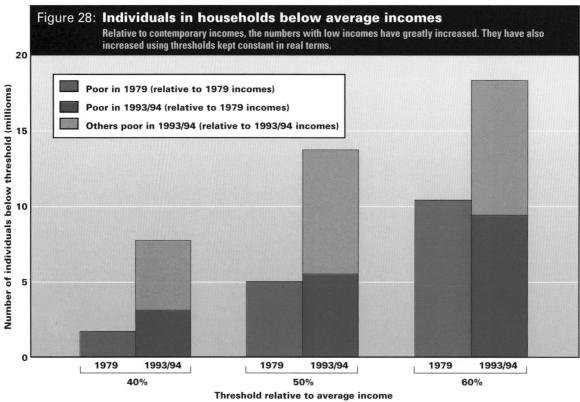

Figure 28: Individuals in households below average incomes

Relative to contemporary incomes, the numbers with low incomes have greatly increased. They have also increased using thresholds kept constant in real terms.

Number of individuals below threshold (millions)

Legend:
- Poor in 1979 (relative to 1979 incomes)
- Poor in 1993/94 (relative to 1979 incomes)
- Others poor in 1993/94 (relative to 1993/94 incomes)

Threshold relative to average income: 40%, 50%, 60% (each with 1979 and 1993/94)

Source: DSS (1996). Incomes are after housing costs.

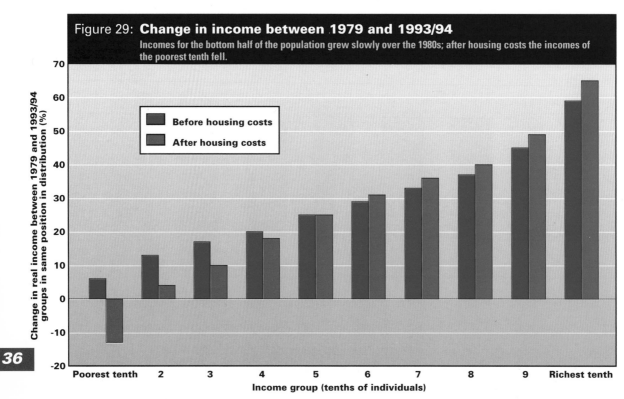

Figure 29: Change in income between 1979 and 1993/94

Incomes for the bottom half of the population grew slowly over the 1980s; after housing costs the incomes of the poorest tenth fell.

Change in real income between 1979 and 1993/94 groups in same position in distribution (%)

Legend:
- Before housing costs
- After housing costs

Income group (tenths of individuals): Poorest tenth, 2, 3, 4, 5, 6, 7, 8, 9, Richest tenth

Source: DSS (1996).

society) would argue that the figures *over*-state any rise in poverty, since the safety net itself is, for some, higher in real terms than it was. Those taking a 'relative' view would argue that they *under*-state the rise, since the level of the safety net has fallen behind contemporary living standards.

The second series - 'Households Below Average Income' - can be analysed from either perspective. **Figure 28** shows that, in 1979, 1.7 million individuals had incomes (allowing for family circumstances and after allowing for housing costs) below 40 per cent of that year's average. By 1993/94, 7.7 million people had incomes below 40 per cent of the average for those two years; of these, 3.1 million had incomes below 40 per cent of *1979 average income*. If 50 per cent is taken as the threshold, the rise is from 5.0 to 13.7 million (with 5.5 million of these below half the 1979 average).

If these thresholds are used to measure poverty relative to contemporary living standards, the numbers affected increased more than four-fold (40 per cent of average income) or nearly trebled (50 per cent). Even from an 'absolute' viewpoint using a fixed measuring rod relative to 1979 incomes, the numbers affected increased despite a 40 per cent increase in overall incomes.

These trends are clear whatever the precise definition: the number of people with low incomes increased over the 1980s - substantially so if any kind of relative measuring rod is used.

Figure 29 shows the difference between the real incomes (before and after housing costs)[42] of individuals placed in successive tenths of the populations in 1979 and 1993/94. While average income for the population as a whole rose by 40 per cent, the real income of the bottom tenth rose by only 6 per cent (before housing costs), and *fell* by 13 per cent (AHC).[43] Meanwhile, the incomes of the top tenth rose by 60 per cent.[44]

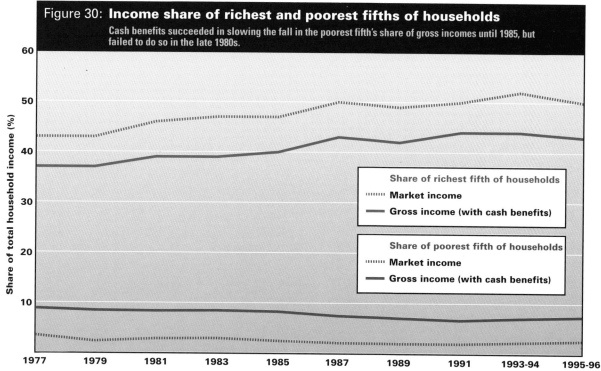

Figure 30: **Income share of richest and poorest fifths of households**

Cash benefits succeeded in slowing the fall in the poorest fifth's share of gross incomes until 1985, but failed to do so in the late 1980s.

Share of total household income (%)

Share of richest fifth of households
Market income
Gross income (with cash benefits)

Share of poorest fifth of households
Market income
Gross income (with cash benefits)

Source: ONS (1997a)
Note: Households ranked by equivalent incomes

Incomes have thus become much less equally distributed in Britain since the late 1970s. **Figure 30** indicates how cash benefits have affected this, showing the shares of original and of gross income received by the poorest and richest fifths of households between 1977 and 1995/96.[45] Over the period, the top fifth increased its share of original (market) income from 43 to 50 per cent. Its smaller share of gross income (after allowing for cash benefits) rose from 37 to 43 per cent.

By contrast, the poorest fifth's share of market income fell from 3.6 to a low point of 2.0 per cent in 1991. Cash benefits boosted its share of gross income, but this still fell from 8.9 to 6.7 per cent. Notably, over the period up to 1985, the reduction in the bottom group's share of gross incomes was less than that of original income; after 1985, the reverse was the case. Over the earlier period, inequality in *market* incomes widened, particularly as unemployment rose. However, the welfare state largely succeeded in blunting the effects of this on the gross incomes of the poorest. In effect, the welfare state was working harder than in the 1970s. After 1985, however, inequality of market incomes continued to widen, but the gap in gross incomes did so faster. In particular, with benefit levels price-linked, the benefit system failed to check the rise in inequality.

By 1995-96, however, the share of the poorest fifth had recovered somewhat, taking its share of gross income back to 7.4 per cent. On these figures, the rapid growth in inequality seen in the 1980s did not continue into the recession and recovery from it in the early 1990s, during which overall income growth was low. It is yet to be seen whether this is a permanent change in trend.

Conclusion

These profound changes do not in themselves prove the need to change the welfare system. They do, however, suggest the need to at least examine alternatives to structures originally set up in a very different world.

Further reading
Family Change and Future Policy, Kathleen Kiernan and Malcolm Wicks (JRF, 1990)

Cohabitation: Extra-marital childbearing and social policy, Kathleen Kiernan and Valerie Estaugh (FPSC, 1993; JRF Social Policy Research *Findings* No. 37)

Lone Parent Families in the UK, Jonathan Bradshaw and Jane Millar (HMSO, 1991)

One-parent Families: Policy options for the 1990s, Louie Burghes (JRF, 1993)

Social Change and Social Policy: New challenges to the Beveridge model, edited by Sally Baldwin and Jane Falkingham (Harvester Wheatsheaf, 1994), especially Chapter 1, 'Social insurance and poverty alleviation: an empirical analysis' by Steven Webb

'Beveridge and his assumptive worlds: The incompatibilities of a flawed design', Howard Glennerster and Martin Evans in J. Hills, J. Ditch and H. Glennerster (eds) *Beveridge and Social Security: An international retrospective* (Oxford, 1994)

Households Below Average Income 1979-1993/94, Department of Social Security (HMSO, 1996)

Income and wealth: Volume 1, Report, chaired by Sir Peter Barclay (JRF, 1995)

Income and wealth: Volume 2, A survey of the evidence, John Hills (JRF, 1995)

New Inequalities: The changing distribution of income and wealth in the UK, edited by John Hills (Cambridge, 1996)

Policy options: service by service

2

Social security as a whole

Britain's social security system is complex. Nearly half the total consists of benefits like the retirement pension depending on people's national insurance contribution records. One-third, like Income Support, depends on both circumstances and assessed means. The remainder, like Child Benefit, depends on circumstances alone (**Figure 31**). Spending on elderly people takes nearly half the total and almost one-quarter goes to sick or disabled people.

The system includes at least 37 separate benefits; the two comprehensive guides to its rules published by the Child Poverty Action Group together have over 950 pages; over 100,000 people are employed to run it; its administration cost £3.5 billion in 1996-97.[1]

There is not enough space in a report of this kind to analyse such a complex system and

reform proposals in detail; there is a wealth of material in the 'further reading' listed below and elsewhere. Instead, in this section we look at some of the broad options and issues affecting social security as a whole, while in the next we concentrate on the largest part of the total, pensions. The eight issues examined in this section are:

(a) Private sector alternatives;
(b) Greater means-testing;
(c) Tax-benefit integration;
(d) Basic incomes;
(e) The contributory principle;
(f) Individual versus family benefits;
(g) Generosity and adequacy; and
(h) Getting claimants back into work.

In such a broad examination, it must be remembered that complexity is not always an historical accident. It also results from benefits

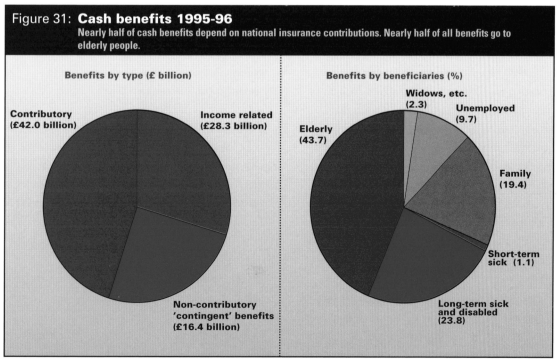

Figure 31: **Cash benefits 1995-96**
Nearly half of cash benefits depend on national insurance contributions. Nearly half of all benefits go to elderly people.

Benefits by type (£ billion)

Contributory (£42.0 billion)

Income related (£28.3 billion)

Non-contributory 'contingent' benefits (£16.4 billion)

Benefits by beneficiaries (%)

Widows, etc. (2.3)

Unemployed (9.7)

Elderly (43.7)

Family (19.4)

Short-term sick (1.1)

Long-term sick and disabled (23.8)

39

Source: DSS (1997)

tailored to complex and highly varied circumstances. Rationalisation proposals often face the choice between rougher justice and losses for some (as elements catering for special needs are cut out) or greater costs if simpler benefits are set high enough to cover special needs (hence increasing generosity for 'ordinary' cases). Only by detailed analysis can such problems be fully investigated.

Similarly, there are inevitable trade-offs between different objectives. Providing incomes to those out of work necessarily affects their incentive to get work. Unless they are left destitute some kind of disincentive is unavoidable. The issue is where the trade-offs are struck.

(a) Private sector alternatives

If social security *only* redistributed from rich to poor, there might be little argument for expanding the private sector's role. Charity could replace some state redistribution, but it is unlikely that this would be on a substantial scale.

However, the role of the system goes much wider. Substantial parts of its effect are as *insurance* and as a *'savings bank'* (pp 15-21). In principle, either role could be fulfilled privately. Indeed, the private sector already has a substantial role in occupational pensions. The question is the appropriate balance between state and private provision, and within private provision the balance between compulsory employer and voluntary personal arrangements.

Topping the agenda of those who would like to shift the balance much more towards the private sector are:

● Abolition of the State Earnings Related Pension Scheme;
● Encouragement of 'contracting out' from the basic retirement pension, unemployment and

invalidity insurance to use private alternatives;
● Private insurance to protect mortgages and against risks of needing long-term residential care.

Three issues are raised by such proposals:
● Private insurers may not be able to judge the risks people face as well as the individuals themselves. If this is so, insurers have to pitch their terms on the assumption that only 'bad risks' will seek cover (for example, for unemployment insurance, those who know they may well lose their jobs; for retirement annuities, those who believe they will live a long time). Private insurance gives a worse deal for the ordinary person in such cases - technically called 'adverse selection' - than the 'pooled' coverage given by social insurance.[2]

● With social insurance providing minimum coverage, the State collects 'premiums' which balance out good and bad risks. On the other hand, with private insurance but a state-guaranteed minimum income (like Income Support), the Government will find itself without the premiums but picking up all of the 'downside risk', where, for instance, some private pension schemes perform poorly or where individuals fail to make minimum provision for retirement.[3]

● We already have a 'Pay as You Go' system in place, under which one generation effectively pays for the basic pensions (and health care) of its parents. Switching to a system under which private funds are built up for this coverage ends up with one 'transition' generation paying twice - once for its parents through Pay As You Go and once for itself through private contributions. This is unavoidable, even if the change is phased over decades.

Further problems are related to what is known as 'moral hazard' - knowing they are insured, people may behave more reckessly, or even deliberately incur a risk. However, this problem only makes the case for public insurance if the public sector is better at policing potential abuse than private insurers. Yarrow (1993) suggests that this problem may best be dealt with by increased use of friendly societies. Not only are they better adapted to policing abuse by members, but their traditional users are in precisely the income groups who fall above means-tested support, but make little use of private insurance and pensions.

(b) Greater means-testing

The extent of means-testing has steadily expanded since the War - more than 10 per cent of the population now claim Income Support (**Figure 32**); including their partners and families, more than 17 per cent depend on it. In 1993/94, 22 per cent of the population were in households receiving either Income Support or Housing/Council Tax Benefit.[4]

None the less, some benefits - notably Child Benefit, the state pension, and Unemployment Benefit for some - do go to people unaffected by means-testing. It is therefore argued that further means-testing would allow the spending involved to be better 'targeted':

> 'The eventual elimination of universal benefits would free up sizeable sums of money to be spent on people who need the money most. A substantial reduction in the overall cost of welfare spending could also be made.' (No Turning Back Group of Conservative MPs, 1993, p.22)

Such proposals have to be assessed in the light of the issues explored in the first part of this report:[5]

• 'Universal' benefits do not go indiscriminately to all, but are 'targeted' on those in particular circumstances, meeting wider aims than just poverty relief.

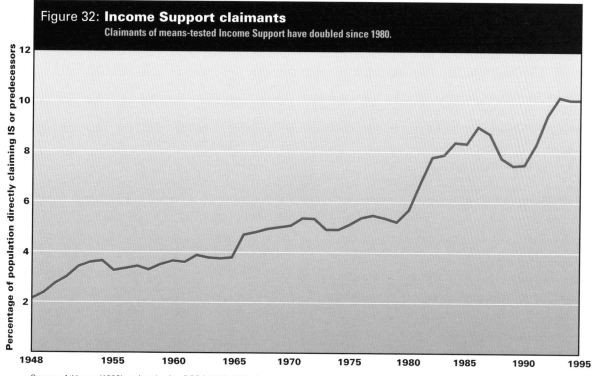

Figure 32: **Income Support claimants**
Claimants of means-tested Income Support have doubled since 1980.

y-axis: Percentage of population directly claiming IS or predecessors

x-axis: 1948 1955 1960 1965 1970 1975 1980 1985 1990 1995

Source: Atkinson (1993) updated using DSS (1997), Table 6

• The *net* effect of tax-financed benefits is redistributive towards those with low incomes, even without means-testing. Reducing 'universal' benefits in order to keep down taxes delivers net gains to those with *high* incomes, the reverse of what is often suggested (see pp 16-17).

• Further means-testing may exacerbate the disincentive effects discussed in pages 22-29, not just for the claimant, but also for partners. In some cases, its effect may be to *increase* the cost to the State, as people end up fully dependent on state support, rather than opting to work more or save more in addition to non-means-tested support.

• Means-testing is expensive: in 1995-96 administration represented 1.1 per cent of costs for retirement pensions, 2.2 per cent for Child Benefit, 9.0 per cent for Income Support, and 36.7 per cent for the Social Fund.[6]

Some of these problems could be lessened if the income level at which benefits were withdrawn was set at a high level, rather than a low one. If the main objection is, for instance, to Child Benefit going to high-income middle-class mothers (even though they are net losers as a result of the taxes they pay to finance it), it would be possible to set up a high-income clawback via the tax system. This might have political advantages, although it would not save a great deal of money, unless 'high income' included the average earner.

(c) Tax-benefit integration

At least four agencies assess incomes for taxes and benefits: the Inland Revenue (income tax), the Contributions Agency (NICs), the Benefits Agency (Income Support and Family Credit), and local authorities (Housing and Council Tax Benefit). Someone in low-paid work claiming Family Credit and Housing Benefit could be on the books of all four at once.

Given that these systems are about deciding the size of transfers in one or other direction between State and individual, it is natural to ask whether these different systems could be combined in a 'one-stop' computerised process. Depending on the answer, people would either pay net tax, or receive a net benefit (sometimes called 'negative income tax'), rather than perhaps paying tax while receiving benefit.[7] This was one of the areas first identified for review by the new Labour Government in 1997.

In assessing such proposals, issues to be addressed include:

• Benefit and tax assessments have different purposes and cover different periods. Income Support makes up income shortfalls in any given week - people need the money *now* - but income tax is, for reasons of fairness, worked out on an annual basis. Integration could mean compromising on one or the other.

• The worst of the overlap of competing income assessments is relatively small - 800,000 Family Credit recipients, compared to over 20 million income taxpayers, for instance. For most taxpayers, income tax and NICs are assessed by employers through the Pay As You Earn (PAYE) system. To redesign PAYE so that employers collected information on *everyone's* family circumstances and housing costs could result in more unnecessary effort than the current duplications of income assessment.

• Benefits and taxes may go to and from different household members. Child Benefit and Family Credit usually go to mothers, for instance. Integration might mean that they would go via the husband's wage packet. With equal sharing within the household, there might be no problem. Where income is *not* equally shared, however, women would lose out.

(d) Basic incomes

At the opposite end of the spectrum from proposals for fully means-tested social security, but closely related to some ideas for tax-benefit integration, are those to replace both means-tested benefits and tax allowances with 'basic incomes' (sometimes known as social dividends or citizens' incomes).[8] Everyone would receive a flat-rate benefit payment of a certain size, but all income would be taxable (except perhaps for a small amount of earnings). In effect, all benefits would be universal, and all 'targeting' would be achieved through the tax system. The replacement of Family Allowances and Child Tax Allowances by Child Benefit could be seen as a move towards such a system.

Such proposals have four key advantages:
- administrative simplicity;
- elimination or substantial reduction of poverty and unemployment traps;
- the potential for significant redistribution towards those with low incomes if the basic incomes were high enough (and take-up would also almost certainly be higher); and
- enhancement of the 'citizenship' - or social solidarity - advantages of all universal benefits.

The problem lies in the marginal tax rates which would be involved. Basic income schemes remove the 100 per cent 'tax' rates of Income Support and the almost equally high rates within the poverty trap. They do this, in effect, by spreading out withdrawal of net benefits over a wider income range. This means higher marginal tax rates for much of the working population - estimates range from at least 50 per cent to over 80 per cent.[9] This would be a substantial jump from the current combined income tax and NIC rate of 33 per cent affecting most workers. Without a substantial change in the political climate, such full-blown schemes do not seem very realistic.

More feasibly, perhaps as a first phase, under 'partial basic incomes' payments to all would replace all of the value of income tax allowances and part (but not all) of existing benefits. This approach could remove some of the effects of poverty and unemployment traps without such substantial increases in tax rates.

Atkinson (1993) suggests using the idea behind partial basic incomes *in combination* with, rather than instead of, insurance benefits. Together, he argues, they could give a guaranteed minimum income for most of the population while minimising reliance on means-testing. In his model, the partial basic incomes would not, however, be unconditional, but would be a 'participation income' paid to those contributing to society in some way - either through work, or availability for work, or through alternatives such as education, caring, or approved voluntary work. This would avoid some of the criticisms of benefits paid out to people manifestly not 'participating' in such ways.

(e) The contributory principle

The 1942 Beveridge Report was rooted in the idea that people would pay contributions into the national insurance system when at work; in return they would be entitled to insurance benefits at times of need. Beveridge's aspiration was that the level of contributions would have an actuarial relationship with the benefits paid out. Contributions were also to be *flat rate*; higher and lower earners would pay the same and - if their contribution records were equivalent - receive the same.

Social security has departed in many aspects from Beveridge's original proposals, but half of all benefits paid out still depend - often in complicated ways - on people's contribution records. Fifty years on, the whole idea of the 'contributory principle' is being questioned, both by those who would like means-testing to be extended and by those who want to widen entitlement to benefits beyond those with good employment records. Problems with the system include:

● The link between contributions and entitlements is obscure, and certainly does not match any clear actuarial principles.

● The simple world of the insured full-time male breadwinner covered by Beveridge's plan has disappeared (see pp 30-38). As a result, new groups have emerged without a good enough record to qualify for contributory benefits, and hence needing means-tested benefits. Tightening of contribution conditions has had a similar effect on those who previously qualified.[10]

● Levels of insurance benefits have never, in fact, been set high enough by themselves to keep people above the state safety net, once one allows for housing costs.[11]

● In effect, NICs have become part of the direct tax system, but features like the Upper Earnings Limit (UEL, beyond which contributions do not increase) create an irrational direct tax structure. Also, only a limited part of personal incomes is subject to NICs (and price-linking of the UEL is steadily reducing its size). As a result, future increases in the cost of contributory pensions are scaled up to imply much larger prospective increases in NIC rates, rather than the cost being spread over all incomes.

● In order to widen the coverage of insurance benefits, certain groups who have not, in fact, contributed are none the less 'credited in'. This avoids some of the problems of basing entitlement only on employment conditions, but means that the contributory principle is already substantially compromised.

These problems are serious. However, the case for abolition is not unchallenged:

● While in actuarial terms, the link between contributions and benefits is obscure and imperfect, much of the welfare system *does* consist of people paying contributions and taxes at one time, in return for benefits they themselves receive at others (see pp 17-21). Ironically, the still fairly widespread belief that people have 'paid their stamps' and expect to receive a return on their payments, while technically incorrect, does reflect the underlying reality.

● NICs are Britain's main manifestation of a 'hypothecated tax', where revenues are earmarked for particular ends. Recent arguments have suggested that *greater* reliance on hypothecation would both be good for democracy and would bridge the mismatch between opinion surveys - which suggest people would like higher spending and higher taxes - and voting behaviour - which suggests they do not trust politicians to spend extra revenues in the ways they would like.[12]

● As a corollary, insurance benefits have a legitimacy, and lack of stigma, which means that take-up is higher - the DSS believes close to 100 per cent[13] - and that they are more successful in reaching all of those for whom they are intended.

● Social insurance emerged in Britain and elsewhere in Europe because of the positive function it plays within the labour market and in relations within industry, functions which it still performs (see pp 28-29).[14]

Putting all this together, while there is clearly a case against the contributory system - particularly that it leaves holes which have to be covered in other ways - there are equally strong arguments that enough of its advantages still hold for it to remain a useful component of the overall system.

(f) Individual versus family benefits

Some parts of social security - in particular, contributory benefits - depend on *individual* circumstances, while others - including all the means-tested benefits - depend on the situation of a family taken as a whole.[15] The tax system is now largely individually based, notably through (almost) independent income tax for husbands and wives introduced from 1990. A key argument for independent taxation was that it was no longer appropriate to view wives as dependants of their husbands, which was the basis of the previous system. Similar arguments could be applied to benefits. 'Family' benefits require careful definitions of what constitutes a 'family' - a task which is far more difficult than it was.

Esam and Berthoud (1991) investigated the effects of bringing similar principles of independence into the benefit system. A first conclusion was that full independence - allowing individuals to claim means-tested

Income Support on the basis of their own income alone (ignoring that of partners) – would be hugely expensive, requiring a 7 pence increase in income tax rates to pay for it. Financed in that way, poor households would, however, tend to gain, and richer ones (such as two-earner couples) to lose.

They analysed alternatives giving more limited independence, for instance, through a means-tested 'personal benefit' payable to those whose own income fell short of a level set below individual Income Support rates. This could be relatively cheap (and would be progressive), but would tend to reduce incentives for married women to take up jobs. Alternatively, a benefit could go to all individuals regardless of income in much the same way as a partial basic income, avoiding the disincentives, but at higher cost.

This analysis highlights a contradiction in the recent evolution of the taxes and benefits. The tax system, and the treatment of those with

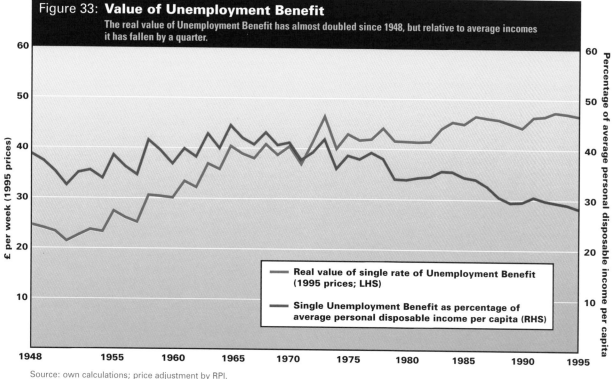

Figure 33: **Value of Unemployment Benefit**
The real value of Unemployment Benefit has almost doubled since 1948, but relative to average incomes it has fallen by a quarter.

Source: own calculations; price adjustment by RPI.

45

higher incomes, has been moving towards greater independence in its treatment of men and women. By contrast, the benefit system, through the much wider use of means-testing, has been moving in exactly the opposite direction in the State's treatment of men and women with lower incomes.

(g) Generosity and adequacy

As an indicator of the value of parts of the benefit system, **Figure 33** shows the value since 1948 of Unemployment Benefit (now non-means tested Job Seekers Allowance) for a single person. In real terms, its value increased through the 1950s and 1960s, reaching a peak in 1973, which was almost as high as its 1995 value. However, relative to general living standards (as measured by personal disposable income), its peak value was reached in 1965 and its relative value in 1995 was only 72 per cent of that in 1948. For most of the period up to 1987, the single person's rate of Supplementary Benefit followed a similar course. However, Income Support rates for single people fell below UB rates in the 1980s, particularly for those under 25. (Figure 35 below shows related trends for the basic pension.)

Taking an 'absolute' measure of generosity, benefit levels have therefore almost doubled since 1948. Taking a 'relative' view, there was slow improvement in the first half of the period, followed by significant decline.

Since Beveridge, the objectives of social security have never been set out in a way allowing measurement of whether benefit levels are 'adequate' to meet their aims. Even Beveridge's proposals, billed as setting rates which would avoid poverty according to Rowntree's pre-War measures of the poverty line, in reality failed to do so; the post-War rates actually set fell short of his proposals in real terms.[16]

Various attempts have been made to provide a measure of adequacy. The Family Budget Unit has recently constructed a series of budgets which would allow families - in the researchers' view - to achieve either a 'modest but adequate' standard of living or to afford a 'low cost' budget. The 'low cost' budget allows families to purchase items which two-thirds of respondents to the 1991 'Breadline Britain' national survey described as necessities, plus items which three-quarters of the population have.

The results of this research suggested that 1992-93 Income Support levels were below the amount needed for the 'low cost' budget by about a quarter for a couple with two children or for a lone parent, but were more than enough to meet the standard for a single pensioner council tenant.[17]

This still does not, however, give an 'objective' view of adequacy. Even the 'low cost' budget - based on survey evidence of popular views of what constitute necessities - required a judgement of how high a vote was required for a 'necessity' to qualify. An alternative is to look at whether those living on Income Support and other benefits have enough money to cope without getting into debt or other financial problems. Marsh and McKay found that 30 per cent of lone parents who were out of work and 24 per cent of families out of work had three or more out of six potential indicators of financial stress, compared to between 4 and 6 per cent of those with 'moderate' incomes.[18] On this basis over a quarter of those out of work and on benefit were none the less 'in severe hardship'.

(h) Getting claimants back into work

Benefits for those without work may ameliorate their immediate position but they do not solve the problem. A prime aim of social security policy should be for claimants, where possible, to find independent income sources. While the overall level of employment depends on macro-economic factors going beyond the scope of (but highly relevant to) this report, the social security structure may discourage employment under some circumstances.

The position of lone parents is a particular cause for concern (see pp 26-28). In response, Burghes (1993) and Holtermann (1993) examined a range of measures which might assist more lone parents to increase their incomes from work. Suggestions include:

• Greater availability of publicly funded childcare, particularly for primary school age children outside school hours and in holidays.
• Allowing childcare costs as a deduction in calculating income for Income Support and Family Credit. A 'disregard' of this kind was introduced into Family Credit in 1995 and extended by the July 1997 Budget.
• Increasing the 'earnings disregard' for lone parents in calculating Income Support. This would increase the gain from taking jobs for small numbers of hours (but would reduce the gain from working long enough to qualify for Family Credit).
• Adapting the role of the Child Support Agency, so that it paid out 'advanced' or 'guaranteed' maintenance payments - the agency would pay out maintenance and would be responsible for its recovery from absent fathers. This would give a guaranteed (and regular) income in and out of work, reducing the width of the poverty trap (see Figure 19), and increasing the gain from work.

Holtermann suggested that the first two of these, at least, while they would initially increase public spending would in the long run end up in substantial *savings* to the Treasury, as savings on Income Support and tax receipts outweighed the spending on childcare or Family Credit.

Lone parents are a special case, but the principle that there may be long-term savings to the Treasury *and* gains to claimants for allowing more benefits to run on in work has wider applications. An example was the Enterprise Allowance scheme, under which those who had been unemployed could carry on receiving some benefit while establishing a new business. Snower (1993) proposed going about the problem from the other direction: paying subsidies to employers to take on unemployed workers, with the size of subsidy rising with the length of time unemployment has lasted.

Finally, there is the question of whether benefits should run on unconditionally for as long as claimants are out of work. In Beveridge's original proposals, it would have been compulsory for those claiming for over 6 months to "attend a work or training centre". Piachaud (1993) argued that, as part of an extensive programme for returning to full employment:

> *"... for people unemployed for any considerable length of time income be made conditional on work or training. It is patronising sentimentality to oppose all conditions on the receipt of unemployment benefits: what matters is ensuring decent incomes and good quality work or training."*

The 'Welfare to work' measures introduced by the new Labour Government in the July 1997 Budget incorporate both of these last approaches: employers will receive weekly subsidies for taking on the young and long-term unemployed; while young people refusing one of the work or training options open to them will have their benefits suspended.

Summary - key issues in social security

● **Private alternatives and means-testing.** There is a choice between increasing 'targeting' of social security on those with lower incomes through means-testing (while the private sector provides more insurance and 'income smoothing' for those with higher incomes), and using tax-financed 'universal' systems where the targeting is achieved by the tax system and the choice of contingencies covered.

● **Tax-benefit integration options.** Benefit and direct tax systems could be combined to remove duplication of income assessments and perhaps produce a more rational structure. Related options include basic income schemes and variants like partial basic incomes and 'participation incomes'.

● **The contributory principle.** The contributory principle for national insurance benefits could be abandoned on the grounds of its compromised nature, or its advantages could be judged still to outweigh its drawbacks.

● **Adequacy.** Decisions have to be taken on whether benefit rates are high enough to keep claimants out of poverty or need to be increased and on whether future uprating continues to be in relation to prices rather than general living standards.

● **Returning to work.** Social security rules, particularly for means-tested benefits could be changed to increase the net returns from returning to work or increasing earnings. Measures already being introduced, in part at least, include improved childcare, subsidies to employers to take on unemployed workers, and making benefit receipt for the long-term young unemployed conditional on taking up work or training opportunities.

Further reading
Poverty and Social Security, A. B. Atkinson (Harvester Wheatsheaf, 1989)

Incomes and the Welfare State, A. B. Atkinson (Cambridge, 1996)

The Economics of the Welfare State, Nicholas Barr (Weidenfeld and Nicholson, new edition 1993)

Private Welfare Insurance and Social Security: pushing the boundaries, Tania Burchardt and John Hills YPS, 1997)

One-parent Families: Policy options for the 1990s, Louie Burghes (JRF, 1993)

Household budgets and living standards, edited by Jonathan Bradshaw (JRF, 1993)

Social Security Departmental Report, Department of Social Security (Cm 3613, Stationery Office, 1997)

The Reform of Social Security, Andrew Dilnot, John Kay and Nick Morris (Oxford, 1984)

Beveridge and Social Security: An International Retrospective, edited by John Hills, John Ditch and Howard Glennerster (Oxford, 1994)

Independent Benefits for Men and Women, Peter Esam and Richard Berthoud (PSI, 1991; JRF Social Policy Research *Findings* No. 18)

Becoming a Breadwinner: Policies to assist lone parents with childcare, Sally Holtermann (Daycare Trust, 1993)

Reconnecting Taxation, Geoff Mulgan and Robin Murray (DEMOS, 1993)

Who benefits? Reinventing social security, 'No Turning Back' Group of Conservative MPs (Conservative Political Centre, 1993)

Child Tax Allowances? A Comparison of child benefit, child tax reliefs and basic incomes as instruments of family policy, Hermione Parker and Holly Sutherland (STICERD, London School of Economics, 1991; JRF Social Policy Research *Findings* No. 13)

What's wrong with Fabianism?, David Piachaud (Fabian Pamphlet 558, 1993)

Instead of the Dole, Hermione Parker (Routledge, 1989)

What is a Family? Benefit models and social realities, Jo Roll (Family Policy Studies Centre, 1991; JRF Social Policy Research *Findings* No. 19)

The Future of the Welfare State, Dennis Snower (Birkbeck College Discussion Paper 16/92, 1992)

Social Security and Friendly Societies: Options for the future, George Yarrow (National Conference of Friendly Societies, 1993)

State pensions and social security for elderly people

The main elements of social security for elderly people are:

• The **basic pension**, with a full value of £62.45 per week from April 1997 for a single person, or £99.80 for a married couple where the wife does not have her own basic pension. Its size depends on how many years National Insurance Contributions (NICs) were paid in (with years credited for 'home responsibilities').

• The **State Earnings Related Pension Scheme** (SERPS), where - after transition from earlier, more generous rules - people will receive an 'Additional Pension' based on 20 per cent of the average lifetime earnings on which NICs were paid. Most members of occupational pension schemes pay lower NICs in return for the scheme paying pensions which should be at least as great as their SERPS rights. People can also 'contract out' of SERPS by paying minimum

amounts into a personal pension scheme (where size of eventual pension is not guaranteed).

• **Incapacity benefit** (ICB), formerly Invalidity Benefit, paid to people meeting contribution conditions who are off sick for over six months. The basic amount equals the single pension, and people receive additions for dependants and the age the invalidity started. Unlike the old Invalidity Benefit, ICB is taxable and is subject to a more stringent medical test.

• **Income Support** (IS), which is means-tested and makes up pensioners' incomes to a level just above the full basic pension (with additions for older pensioners). IS recipients also receive full Housing Benefit (HB), for instance, covering all of rent and Council Tax. Slightly better off pensioners can receive partial HB. As Figure 20 showed, pensioners may need a significant

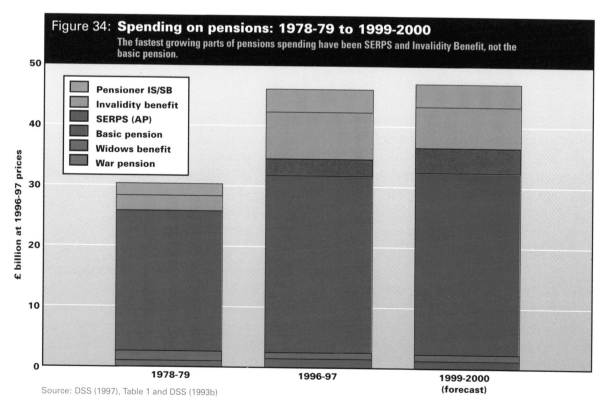

Figure 34: **Spending on pensions: 1978-79 to 1999-2000**
The fastest growing parts of pensions spending have been SERPS and Invalidity Benefit, not the basic pension.

Legend:
- Pensioner IS/SB
- Invalidity benefit
- SERPS (AP)
- Basic pension
- Widows benefit
- War pension

Y-axis: £ billion at 1996-97 prices

X-axis: 1978-79, 1996-97, 1999-2000 (forecast)

Source: DSS (1997), Table 1 and DSS (1993b)

49

amount of extra income above the basic pension to put them clear of means-testing.

Spending

Figure 34 shows spending on the main pension categories (including war and widows' pensions). Between 1978-79 and 1996-97, real spending grew by 52 per cent, 2.4 per cent per year. National income grew more slowly, so the share of GDP represented rose from 5.7 to 6.2 per cent. Apart from the basic pension, the main sources of growth were Invalidity (now Incapacity) Benefit[19] (including for non-pensioners) and payments under SERPS (first made in 1979).

The DSS's projections to 1999-2000 shown in Figure 34 forecast pensions spending rising by only 0.7 per cent annually, thus *falling* to 5.8 per cent of GDP. For the longer term, the OECD (1995) forecasts UK public spending on the main pensions items rising from about 4.5 per cent of GDP in 1991 to a peak of 5.5 per cent in 2035 in contrast to substantial rises in other major economies. This assumes pensions continue to be price-linked.

Equality of pension ages

Pension ages were set at 70 for men and women when state pensions were first introduced in 1908, and reduced to 65 in 1925. In 1940 pension age for women was cut to 60. Official rationales included that wives were younger than husbands but both should retire together, and recognition of women's war work. More cynical observers thought it a "cheap dodge"[20] to head off pressure for pensions at 60 for all, when few women qualified for their own pension. Beveridge kept the inequality.

Under European Community pressure for equal treatment of men and women, the Conservative Government committed itself to equal pension ages in its 1992 election manifesto. It reviewed a number of options,[21] but eventually opted for:

- **Increasing women's pension age to 65**, which will save the Government money compared with current arrangements. By 2035 the net savings could be worth between £2.9 and £5.2 billion at 1991 prices (0.25 - 0.5 per cent of 2035 GDP), depending on whether pensions are price- or earnings-linked in future. Women will receive their pensions five years later than now, although existing pensioners will be unaffected and phasing will protect those born before 1950.[22]

Options which were rejected include:

- **Reducing men's pension age to 60**, which would have avoided upsetting anyone's expectations and could have been seen as a response to increased early retirement (see Figure 25), although it would be strange as a response to longer life-expectancy (Figure 21). By 2035 it would have cost between £3.4 - £6.3 billion at 1991 prices, or 0.3 - 0.6 per cent of GDP (depending on uprating).

- **A common pension age of 63**, which would have split the difference, yielding small net savings to Government.

- **A 'split pension age'**, with either the basic pension or SERPS given at 60, and the other at 65. Giving the basic pension at 60 would benefit those with low lifetime earnings most, but would raise the cost of the basic element, perhaps increasing pressures towards its long-term decline. Giving SERPS at 60, but the basic pension at 65 would exacerbate the tendency of any equalisation to benefit men and penalise women.

- **A 'flexible decade of retirement'**, which would attempt to meet the contradictory increases in life expectancy and early retirement. People could, for instance, retire at 60 with a basic pension fixed at, say, 80 per cent of its normal full value.[23] Alternatively, they could defer until 70 and then receive a pension 80 per cent *higher* than the normal amount, with a sliding scale in between. While flexibility has advantages, there would be big differences between early retirers able to claim ICB and those taking a permanently reduced pension; many of the latter might end up on Income Support.

Uprating policy

Figure 35 shows the value of the basic pension in real terms and relative to average incomes since 1948. Until 1982, the pension was generally increased at least in line with earnings. Since then it has been linked to prices. In real terms, it was nearly 140 per cent more valuable in 1995 than in 1948. However, relative to average (disposable) incomes it reached a peak of 46.8 per cent in 1983, but by 1995 was only 35.6 per cent, nearly a tenth lower than it had been in 1948. The pension is currently worth about 15 per cent of average gross male earnings, lower than at any time since 1971, the earliest date for which this calculation can be made consistently.

With current policies these ratios will continue to fall until the basic pension becomes trivial in relation to contemporary incomes. If earnings growth is 1.5 per cent, by 2040 the pension would be only 7.5 per cent of gross average earnings; if earnings grow by 2 per cent, this ratio would be this low by 2030.

Similar trends affect other benefits. It has to be questioned whether this is sustainable. More than half of pensioners will enjoy occupational or personal pensions in future, but over a third will not. SERPS rights will build up, but those with low lifetime earnings (including groups like the self-employed) will only receive small amounts. Is it feasible to have basic pension and pensioner Income Support levels halved relative to contemporary living standards and expectations? Would we regard a single pension of only £25 - the level it would be with price-linking since 1948 - as acceptable today?

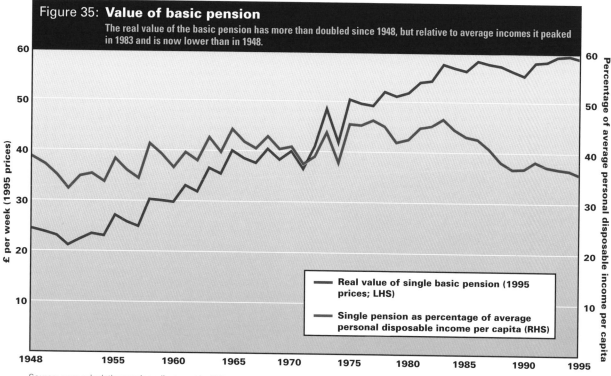

Figure 35: **Value of basic pension**

The real value of the basic pension has more than doubled since 1948, but relative to average incomes it peaked in 1983 and is now lower than in 1948.

£ per week (1995 prices)

Percentage of average personal disposable income per capita

— Real value of single basic pension (1995 prices; LHS)

— Single pension as percentage of average personal disposable income per capita (RHS)

1948   1955   1960   1965   1970   1975   1980   1985   1990   1995

Source: own calculations; price adjustment by RPI.

Figure 36 shows official projections made in 1995 of the gross cost of pensions with either price- or earnings-linking (taking account of the increase in married women's pension age and other effects of the 1995 Pensions Act). Because the key question is *affordability* in terms of the proportion of national income required to pay for pensions through tax or NICs, the costs are shown in relation to GDP (assumed to grow in line with assumed earnings growth of 1.5 per cent and population growth).

If pensions remain price-linked, the proportion of GDP represented grows from 4.4 to 5.0 per cent between 1994 and 2010; by 2040, it is down to 4.2 per cent. However, if an earnings link was restored, the total would be 7.6 per cent in 2040.

• One option would be to **restore some kind of earnings or income link**, accepting an increase in the *net* cost (allowing for effects on tax receipts and other benefits) to be found from tax or NICs

equivalent to about 2.7 per cent of GDP by 2030.[24]

This is not as clearly impossible as some more alarmist coverage implies, particularly by comparison with post-War growth in the British welfare state or the scale of social spending elsewhere in Europe (see Figures 2 and 4). However, it may be that political limits to taxation have already been reached.

• The default option is **to continue to price-link the basic pension**. As Figure 36 shows, the decline in the relative value of the basic pension allows ageing and the growth of SERPS to be accommodated within an almost constant share of GDP.

The end result is, however, a rather strange structure of state pensions. **Figure 37** shows a stylised example of the relationship between average lifetime earnings and state pensions on

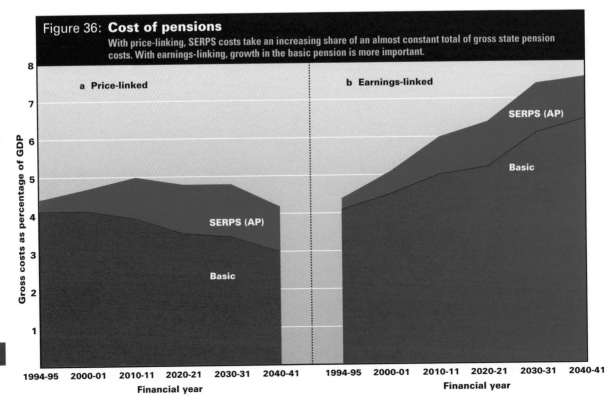

Figure 36: **Cost of pensions**
With price-linking, SERPS costs take an increasing share of an almost constant total of gross state pension costs. With earnings-linking, growth in the basic pension is more important.

a Price-linked

b Earnings-linked

SERPS (AP)

Basic

SERPS (AP)

Basic

Gross costs as percentage of GDP

1994-95   2000-01   2010-11   2020-21   2030-31   2040-41
Financial year

1994-95   2000-01   2010-11   2020-21   2030-31   2040-41
Financial year

Source: Government Actuary (1995)
Note: GDP calculated on assumption that GDP per capita grows in line with 1.5% annual earnings growth assumed by Government Actuary.
Projections take account of 1995 Pensions Act (apportioning savings between basic and additional pensions).

retirement for men retiring in 2040 if price-linking continues with 1.5 per cent earnings growth. For a man earning exactly the male average in each year from 1992 to 2040, his pension on retirement would consist of a basic pension of 7.5 per cent of average earnings in 2040, plus an additional 13.9 per cent from SERPS (or at least as much from an occupational scheme if he was contracted out of SERPS).

Most people would not do as well as this. Seventy per cent of men and women working full-time earn less than the male 'average' in each year. Allowing for this, for years without earnings (for example, in education), and for part-time work, most people would be to the left of Figure 37. People who spent most of their lives in self-employment or poorly paid

part-time work would receive little more than the basic pension - with half its relative value of 1993.

For each subsequent year of retirement, the size of entitlement would be scaled down, as both the minimum given by the basic pension and the maximum payable under SERPS fell behind earnings growth.[25]

Price-linking may therefore keep total state pension costs under control as SERPS matures, but it does so by tilting state pension rights away from those with low lifetime earnings. If the political constraint is on the total pensions budget, SERPS acts as a cuckoo in the nest pushing down the value of the basic pension.

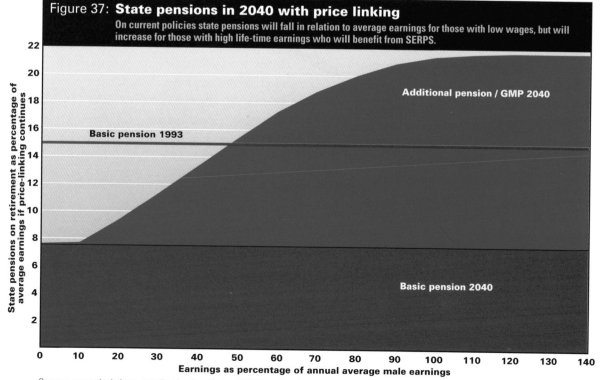

Figure 37: **State pensions in 2040 with price linking**

On current policies state pensions will fall in relation to average earnings for those with low wages, but will increase for those with high life-time earnings who will benefit from SERPS.

State pensions on retirement as percentage of average earnings if price-linking continues

Basic pension 1993

Additional pension / GMP 2040

Basic pension 2040

Earnings as percentage of annual average male earnings

Source: own calculations, not allowing for effects of 1995 Pension Act
Notes: Assumes work for 49 years earning same percentage of average in each year
Basic pension price-linked (1.5% earnings growth)

Alternative structures

If neither the cost of restoring the earnings link nor the kind of structure just outlined are acceptable in the long run, an alternative has to be found. Options include:

● **Abolishing SERPS**. If the cost of SERPS is a main source of the problem, why not simply abandon it and use the savings to maintain the relative value of the basic pension, leaving the private sector to get on with providing income-linked pensions? It is hard to imagine this happening without a long transitional period (protecting accrued rights) and great political difficulties. It would also mean foregoing the advantages which led to the introduction of SERPS - particularly for women and those changing jobs.

● **Means-testing the basic pension**. Dilnot and Johnson (1992) argue that given the growth of both SERPS and of occupational schemes - with 62 per cent of employees and the self-employed members of occupational or personal pension schemes in 1991[26] - a universal state pension is no longer needed. Instead, the resources it uses could be concentrated on the poorest pensioners by setting it at a higher level but means-testing it. This keeps costs under control and raises the safety net in retirement. However, it would extend the 'savings trap' illustrated in Figure 20, undermining the incentive to save or accumulate a private pension for more people than now.

● **A minimum state pension** under which someone's combined basic pension and SERPS rights would not be allowed to fall below a certain percentage of contemporary earnings.[27] If it did, an additional payment would make up the difference. The minimum could be earnings-linked while other elements of the system continued price-linked. The effect would be to maintain the same kind of floor to state pensions as would be achieved by earnings-linking the basic pension (but possibly at a more generous level), but to save public spending as costs were transferred to the private sector as GMPs build up. Unlike means-testing, this would not act as a disincentive to *additional* savings or pension provision. However, by the same token, it would give an incentive to switch away from contracted-out schemes to other forms of pensions or saving. Avoiding this would require employer pension schemes to be made compulsory in some way.

● **Funded pensions**. State pensions in Britain are paid for by current contributions on a 'pay as you go' basis: there is no 'fund' of the kind accumulated by private schemes. It has been suggested that this arrangement can lead to some generations losing out, as they have to pay for the pension promises made to others.[28] Falkingham and Johnson (1993) suggested a 'Universal Funded Pension Scheme' in which everyone would have their own pension fund, invested in the private sector but protected from manipulation by either governments or Maxwell-like employers. The State's role would be to pay "top ups" into the funds of those with earnings too low to produce a reasonable pension. The Conservative Party's 'Basic Pension Plus' proposals made just before it lost the 1997 election had a similar aim, changing the system for those under 25 at the time of introduction.

The bug-bear with any such scheme is how you get there (funding) from here (Pay as You Go). *Either* you set up funds for all now - which means the government has to find impossible sums equivalent to well over a year's national income[29] to cover the accumulated state pension rights people already have - *or* existing rights continue to be paid for out of taxation, but this means that one generation has to pay for pensions twice over (on a PAYG basis for its parents, but building up a fund for itself).

- **Raising pension age.** Willetts (1993) suggests not only equalising pension ages initially at 65, but also then continuing slowly to raise the common pension age to 67. This, he argues, would reflect rising life expectancy and help to 'target' on poorer (generally older) pensioners without means-testing. He also suggests, for the same reasons, a greater addition to pensions at 80 than the current 25p per week.

Summary - key issues in pensions

- **Pension ages.** Men's and women's pension ages are to be equalised at age 65. There are arguments for increasing pension ages to reflect longer lives and to keep down costs but others for reducing them to reflect the increase in early retirement.

- **Uprating policy.** Current policy is for the basic pension not to keep up with general living standards (as it is price-linked only). The issue is whether this is sustainable and whether a restored link with incomes would be affordable.

- **Pension structure.** The cost of state pensions could be reduced in some other way, such as abandoning SERPS or encouraging opting out from or means-testing the basic pension. Further options include setting a minimum to combined state pension rights from either SERPS or the basic pension. State pensions are funded by 'Pay as You Go' finance at present; some proposals suggest switching to a 'funded' system.

Further reading

Invalidity Benefit: Where will the savings come from?, Richard Berthoud (Policy Studies Institute, 1993)

Ageing, Welfare and the Economy, Jane Falkingham and Paul Johnson (Sage, 1992)

Pensions and Divorce, Report of the Independent Working Group chaired by Sir Alec Atkinson (Pensions Management Institute, 1993)

A Unified Funded Pension Scheme (UFPS) for Britain, Jane Falkingham and Paul Johnson (LSE Welfare State Programme Discussion Paper WSP/90, 1993)

The Age of Entitlement, David Willetts (Social Market Foundation, 1993).

Social Justice: Strategies for National Renewal, Social Justice Commission (Vintage, 1994)

Pensions: 2000 and beyond, Retirement Income Inquiry (RII, 1996)

How to Pay for the Future: Building a stakeholders' welfare, Frank Field (Institute of Community Studies, 1996)

Pensions Policy in the UK: An economic analysis, Andrew Dilnot and others (Institute for Fiscal Studies, 1994)

Health services

Public-private boundaries and competition

In the late 1980s there was a fundamental Government review of the National Health Service (NHS). Expanding private health insurance was seriously considered, but rejected. The economic evidence suggested it would be even more expensive, both for the economy and for the public purse. As **Figure 38** shows, Britain's health services are remarkably cheap in international terms (particularly given the relatively large size of its elderly population). Public spending takes 5.8 per cent of GDP compared to the OECD average of 6.0 per cent, and is well below general western European levels. The USA spends a higher proportion of national income on its limited *public* health care system as Britain does on the NHS - and then spends another 8 per cent of GDP privately.

The previous Government opted to try to get more from existing spending by changing the *internal* organisation of the NHS, creating an 'internal' or 'quasi-market', where newly independent providers - **hospital trusts** - bid for contracts from two kinds of purchaser: the District Health Authority (DHA) and **GP fundholders** (GPs with a budget for purchasing non-emergency care and community services for their patients). By April 1996, virtually all NHS provider units were run by about 400 Trusts. More than half of GP practices are now fundholders.[30]

The new Government is committed to reforming the system, but there is still fierce debate about its effects. Did the reforms lead to greater efficiency and more patient choice? Or are some patients gaining favourable treatment at the expense of others while the breakdown of planning has led to

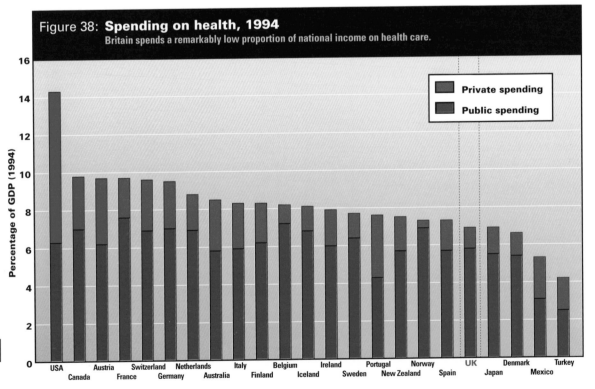

Figure 38: **Spending on health, 1994**
Britain spends a remarkably low proportion of national income on health care.

Private spending
Public spending

Percentage of GDP (1994)

USA Canada Austria France Switzerland Germany Netherlands Australia Italy Finland Belgium Iceland Ireland Sweden Portugal New Zealand Norway Spain UK Japan Denmark Mexico Turkey

Source: OECD database

wasteful duplication and gaps in provision? On the basis of early evidence, independent researchers suggest that there may be some efficiency gains from new arrangements, but also worries about administrative costs and equity problems.[31]

What is clear is that the reforms did not reduce spending - in fact, spending rose in the preparatory and first years of the reforms, partly to pay for the operation of the internal market.

Pressures on public spending

Throughout the 1980s there was a fierce debate over the level of public spending on the NHS. For the Conservatives, spending increased massively in real terms. For the Labour Party when in Opposition, spending failed to keep up with needs. In essence both sides were right. **Figure 39** shows that real public spending on health more than doubled between 1973-74 and 1995-96, and the annual growth rate has been more than 3 per cent since 1978-79.

But this only allows for general inflation. The second line in the figure shows the 'volume' of health resources spending could pay for (for example, numbers of doctors and nurses), adjusting for changes in the specific prices paid by the NHS (for example, doctors' and nurses' pay). Here the growth is less dramatic - 1.8 per cent annually between 1978-79 and 1995-96.

The third line adjusts further for the effects of population ageing to give an index of the resources available in relation to need since 1981-82. Age-related needs expanded almost as rapidly over the 1980s as the volume of NHS resources; at times in the early 1980s, needs were growing *faster* than resources. Add to this the pressures on spending from new technological opportunities, and the move of resources to create greater equity between areas (under the Resource Areas Working Party or 'RAWP' system), and it is small wonder that some people saw decline in the services available relative to needs.

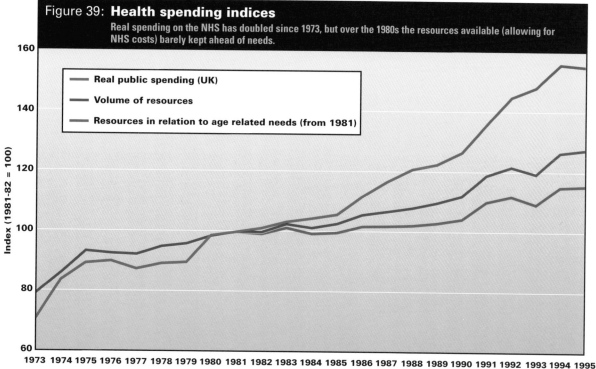

Figure 39: **Health spending indices**

Real spending on the NHS has doubled since 1973, but over the 1980s the resources available (allowing for NHS costs) barely kept ahead of needs.

— Real public spending (UK)

— Volume of resources

— Resources in relation to age related needs (from 1981)

Index (1981-82 = 100)

1973 1974 1975 1976 1977 1978 1979 1980 1981 1982 1983 1984 1985 1986 1987 1988 1989 1990 1991 1992 1993 1994 1995
Financial year starting

Source: Le Grand and Vizard (forthcoming)

In the early 1990s the volume of spending increased faster then age-related needs, and pressures in the immediate future are lower. **Figure 40** shows an index of health spending needs allowing for the changing age structure of the population. In 1981, average spending equalled 124 per cent of that going on someone aged 45-64; by 1991 ageing meant that this ratio had risen to 138. Looking ahead, there is pressure from projected ageing, but over the *twenty-five* years from 1991 it adds up to a smaller increase than over the *ten* years before.[32]

There are other pressures:
• The internal market will highlight additional needs - this is the job of the Districts. As District and GP funding formulae are brought in, equalisation will create 'losers' and, with them, pressure to level up spending, much as happened with the RAWP equalisation between regions in the 1970s and 1980s.

• One reason why the NHS has cost so little in international terms has been its power as an almost monopoly purchaser of doctors. Competition between trusts for the key specialists who can win important contracts may drive up their pay.

• More generally there may be pressure resulting from the way in which NHS pay has failed to keep up with private sector pay. After the large pay awards of the early 1980s, NHS pay per worker fell behind the private sector, although no further ground was lost after 1986. Overall, private sector pay increased by 17 per cent more than the NHS average from 1981-82 to 1993, or by 10 per cent more starting from 1982-83.[33] Periodic 'catch up' pay awards drive up costs, as Figure 39 shows. Without them, however, recruitment standards may fall to unacceptable levels.

• The advance in what is technologically possible creates demands for services which did not previously exist: one 1980s ministerial

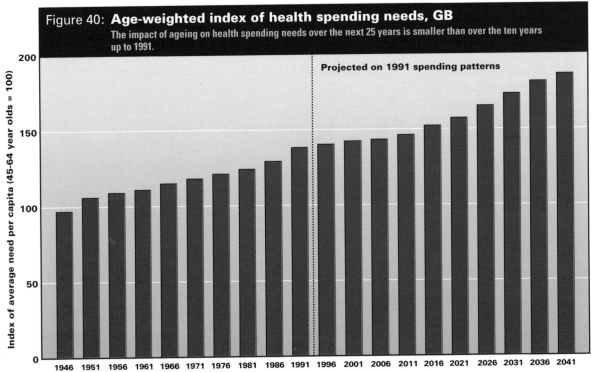

Figure 40: **Age-weighted index of health spending needs, GB**
The impact of ageing on health spending needs over the next 25 years is smaller than over the ten years up to 1991.

Projected on 1991 spending patterns

Index of average need per capita (45-64 year olds = 100)

Source: Hills (1992) updated for revised population projections in OPCS (1993b) and using 'high variation' of spending with age

estimate was that this added 0.5 per cent annually to NHS costs.[34] This may be checked as 'hi tech' solutions come under more critical scrutiny.

Responses to rising costs

The demographic pressures on the NHS over the next few years may not be as severe as in the 1980s. International economic pressures may begin to restrain the costs of technological advance, but expectations *will* rise with standards elsewhere in the economy. A number of responses are possible:

• Continuing with the current basic system, accepting that there will be slow but steady upward pressure on the resources needed from taxation or reductions in other spending.

• Further extending the range of services for which charges are made. Charges reached 4.5 per cent of NHS finance in England in 1989-90, up from just over two per cent in 1978-79, but fell to 2.3 per cent in 1995-96.[35] Options which have reached the public agenda include 'hotel charges' for hospital occupancy. Others could include charging for GP consultations, as already is done for prescriptions, and has already been taken much further for dentistry and opticians.

• Given the system under which certain groups, including recipients of Income Support, are exempted from prescription charges, extension of this kind of charging is, in effect, an extension of means-testing. The switch from long-stay geriatric wards to the use of residential care, sometimes covered by Income Support (or now through local authorities) has a similar effect. In theory, means-testing could be taken much further - for instance, those with incomes above a certain level could be required to take out private insurance. It would raise, in an extreme form, all the general issues connected with means-testing discussed earlier in this report.

• Alternatively, the costs of the NHS could be made more apparent to taxpayers through earmarking - or at least, clearer labelling - of part of income tax as going to the NHS, or even through introduction of an 'NHS tax'. The trade-off between health spending and tax levels would then be more explicit. People might be prepared to vote for higher taxes if they knew they were going to the NHS. Alternatively, preferences against higher taxes might be stronger and people would see directly that these were incompatible with higher health spending. Either way, democratic choices could be more clearly expressed.[36]

Equity

One aim of the health service is equal treatment for equal need; whether it achieves this has been controversial. **Figure 41** gives an indicator of access to the main 'gate-keepers' of the system. The left-hand panel shows the proportion of the population consulting a doctor within the previous two weeks by income group.[37] The overall proportion visiting their GP rose from 12.1 to 16.0 per cent between 1974 and 1994, and the gradient in favour of lower income groups steepened (this is consistent with the distribution of wider health spending shown in Figure 9 above).

Such a pattern may or may not reflect variations in *need*. Lacking objective evidence, we can look at people who report *themselves* as having an illness limiting their activity. More people described themselves as sick in 1994 than in 1974 (although we do not know whether this reflects an iller population or a less stoical one). The right-hand panel shows the proportion of these consulting a doctor. The overall rise in consultations is small, from 32.1 to 33.0 per cent, but there is a clearer tilting towards those with lower incomes. There is certainly no evidence here of a pro-rich bias in access to health care.

A more sophisticated study[38] found no consistent impact of economic circumstances on use of primary health care. For elderly men, low incomes were associated, other circumstances being equal, with *reduced* use of GPs. For elderly women, the opposite was true.

These findings suggest that the NHS has been more successful in eliminating barriers to entry than most other health care systems, and more successful than critics give it credit for.

Quite distinct from inequalities in health care are inequalities in *health* -particularly in age-at-death for different groups and regions.[39] Substantial differences remain. If one looks at the population as a whole, inequalities in ages-at-death *narrowed* over the period 1974 to 1985.[40]

However, looking at consistent areas (county/district level), proportionate differences in mortality rates for under-65s between 'best' and 'worst' areas widened between 1950 and 1990. The high mortality areas were also those with high scores in terms of deprivation.[41]

Preventive health measures

Given that the aims of health policy should focus on *health* rather than *health care*, issues in the debate go much wider than just the state of the NHS. The *Health of the Nation* White Paper published in 1992 was a recognition of the importance of 'preventive health measures'. The principal difficulty here is that many of the relevant 'measures' are not under the control of the NHS. Controls on advertising of harmful products, like tobacco and alcohol, and tax increases on them (in tobacco's case, raising distributional issues); changing the nation's diet and exercise habits; improving its accident record: all come under different ministries. There is a problem of ministerial co-ordination, at the very least.

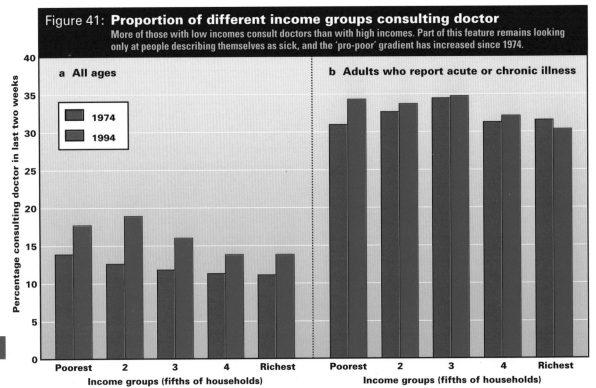

Figure 41: **Proportion of different income groups consulting doctor**
More of those with low incomes consult doctors than with high incomes. Part of this feature remains looking only at people describing themselves as sick, and the 'pro-poor' gradient has increased since 1974.

Source: Le Grand, Winter and Woolley (1990) Tables 4.12 and 4.14 updated (based on GHS data)

Summary - key issues in health services

• **The evolution of the internal market.**
Whether GP fundholding and trust status for 'provider' units produced efficiency improvements and, if so, whether this was at the expense of equity in access to treatment is still fiercely debated.

• **Continuing pressures on spending.**
Demographic pressures on NHS costs will be less strong than in the 1980s, but these and other pressures will still be upwards. This prompts the questions of whether funding should continue to be overwhelmingly from general taxation or from alternatives, such as an earmarked 'NHS tax' or from more charges on those with higher incomes.

• **Preventive health.** The 1992 White Paper has increased the emphasis placed on preventive health measures, but policy responses need to come largely in areas outside the control of the health department.

Further reading

'The National Health Service: Safe in Whose Hands?', Julian Le Grand, David Winter and Frances Woolley in J. Hills (ed) *The State of Welfare* (Oxford, 1990)

Implementing GP Fundholding: Wild card or winning hand? Howard Glennerster, Manos Matsaganis, and Patricia Owens (Open University, 1994)

Unhealthy Societies: The afflictions of inequality, Richard Wilkinson (Routledge, 1996)

Death in Britain: How local mortality rates have changed: 1950s -1990s, Daniel Dorling (JRF, 1997)

Evaluating NHS Reforms, edited by Ray Robinson and Julian Le Grand (King's Fund Institute, 1994)

The Health of the Nation, Department of Health (HMSO, 1992)

The Health of the Nation: The BMJ View, British Medical Journal (1993)

Education

Qualification levels

Although education has more to offer than the achievement of qualifications,[42] much current debate reflects worries that standards are falling and too few young people gain qualifications.

In fact, the qualifications of the population are clearly improving. Between 1979 and 1995, the proportion of school-leavers achieving five or more GCSE passes at Grade C or better (i.e. equivalent to O level) rose from 24 to 45 per cent. The proportion of young people obtaining one or more A level rose from 18 to 34 per cent between 1979 and 1995, and obtaining three or more A levels from 9 to 23 per cent.[43]

These continuing improvements are working their way through into the labour force. **Figure 42** shows the qualifications in 1994 of those born in successive decades since 1925.

At all levels the picture is one of continuous improvement.

In addition, the level of qualifications has become *less* dependent on parental occupation and home background. For instance, the chances of someone with a professional or managerial father having a degree were 2.7 times those for the population as a whole in 1974, but only 1.8 times as high in 1990. For lower qualifications, the differentials were smaller.[44]

State schools and universities have gradually been achieving the goals set by the reforms of the 1940s and 1960s, but not as fast as our competitors. The international comparisons in **Figure 43** present a more alarming picture. Fewer than 30 per cent of young people in England obtained Grade C or better passes in maths, science and English or obtained two or

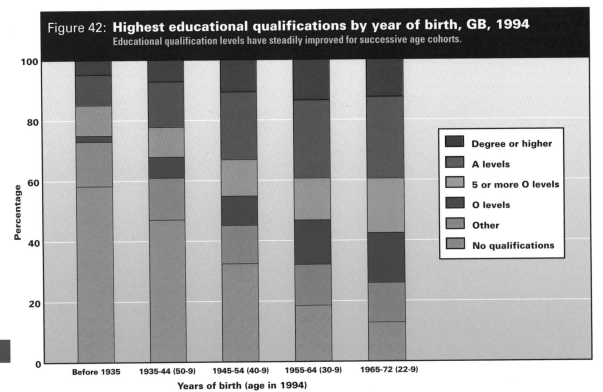

Figure 42: **Highest educational qualifications by year of birth, GB, 1994**
Educational qualification levels have steadily improved for successive age cohorts.

Source: Glennerster and Low (1990), Table 3A.7 updated (using GHS data).

more A levels in 1990-91. Equivalent levels (using their national languages and higher education entrance requirements) were reached by 48 per cent or more in the other three countries. The 56 per cent of 16-19 year olds in education or training in England is much lower than in the other countries, although the situation has improved since 1990-91.

Public spending

As with health, the UK spends a smaller proportion of its national income on public education than the OECD average - 5.1 per cent compared to 5.8 per cent in 1993. However, **Figure 44** shows that this proportion is above that in Japan and Germany.

In contrast to social security and health, the purely demographic pressures on education spending are easing. Figure 21 above shows that the proportion of the population aged under 16 is forecast to rise slightly between 1991 and 2001, but then to decline slowly for the next forty years. The picture presented in Figure 5 suggests that with the age structure of 2041 but unchanged spending at a given age, total education spending per head of population would be 11 per cent *lower* than with the actual age structure of 1991.

As with the NHS, the bulk of education spending goes on pay. Again, changes in pay per education worker fell behind the private sector in the early 1980s, by 6 per cent up to 1993 starting from either a 1981-82 or 1982-83 base.[45] Catching up would be costly but, without it, quality may fall.

The main pressures come from policy objectives that reflect the kinds of international comparisons shown in Figure 43. The previous Government's aim was for one-third of young people to be entering higher education by the year 2000. By 1994-95, new entrants to higher education had risen from 14.6 to over 30 per cent of 18-19 year olds since 1987-88.[46]

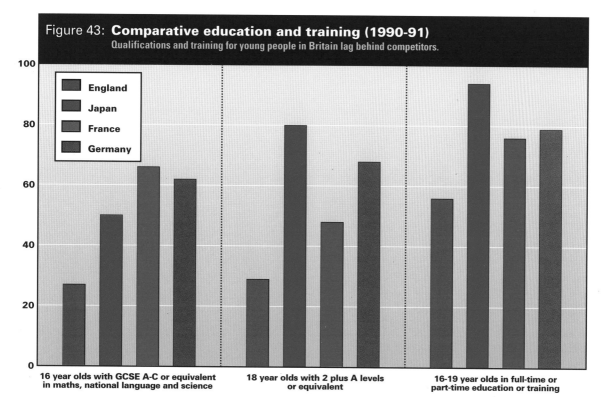

Figure 43: **Comparative education and training (1990-91)**
Qualifications and training for young people in Britain lag behind competitors.

Legend: England, Japan, France, Germany

16 year olds with GCSE A-C or equivalent in maths, national language and science

18 year olds with 2 plus A levels or equivalent

16-19 year olds in full-time or part-time education or training

Source: Green and Steedman (1993)

However, this expansion has not been accompanied by an equivalent increase in the resources going to higher education. In contrast to the rise in resources per head of the school age population, particularly at primary school (**Figure 45**), the volume of resources (with spending adjusted for education prices like lecturers' pay) going to post-school education fell in relation to the size of the relevant age group during the 1980s. In the early 1990s the resources going to post-school education for those aged 19-24 rose by 40 per cent. Given the more rapid rise in participation rates, this did not, however, mean a rise in the resources *per student*. In fact real funding per student *fell* by 17 per cent between 1991-92 and 1995-96.[47]

Options for higher education funding
This situation implies a number of choices:

- Continuing as we are, with rising student numbers and falling resources per student.
- Increasing resources in line with the growth in student numbers, implying increased spending to be financed from taxation.
- Finding new ways of increasing the resources for higher education, particularly from its direct beneficiaries.

It is on the last option that attention has recently been focused. The debate starts from the observation that most students obtaining degrees end up with substantially higher incomes than people without degrees. In contrast to other parts of the welfare state, higher education gives net benefits to those with high lifetime incomes even after one allows for the greater tax bills they face. This suggests a case for changing the whole basis of higher education funding to protect standards without abandoning expansion.

The main alternatives are:
- The traditional grant system, which had least adverse effects on incentives, but had high tax costs.

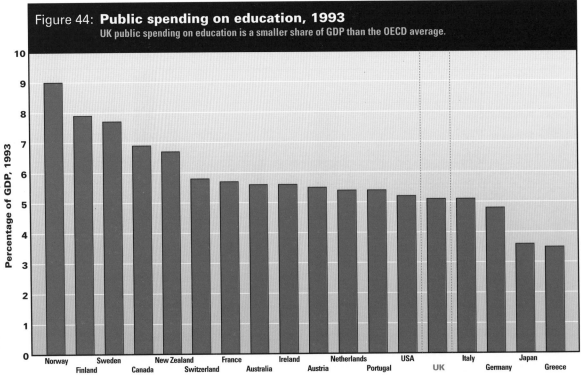

Figure 44: **Public spending on education, 1993**
UK public spending on education is a smaller share of GDP than the OECD average.

Percentage of GDP, 1993

Norway, Finland, Sweden, Canada, New Zealand, Switzerland, France, Australia, Ireland, Austria, Netherlands, Portugal, USA, UK, Italy, Germany, Japan, Greece

Source: OECD (1996a)

• Loans systems run on conventional 'mortgage' type lines (like the new 'top up' loans), which have relatively high administrative costs and default rates and which may act as a deterrent to entry for those who think they may not end up with high earnings (even if the average student does).

• A graduate tax, under which higher education would be free and maintenance grants paid, but in return recipients would be subject to an addition to the rate of National Insurance Contributions paid throughout their subsequent working lives.

• An income-contingent loan system, under which repayments would be collected as a percentage of earnings through the NIC system as with a graduate tax, but would only continue until the original loan (at a zero real interest rate) had been paid off. Barr and Falkingham (1993) conclude this offers the best option for increasing the resources available to higher education, while minimising disincentives to enter it, defaults and administration costs. The Dearing Committee on

higher education recommended a system of this kind, combined with partial student fees, when it reported in July 1997. The Government indicated that it plans to bring in a variant of Dearing's proposals from October 1998.

Vocational training

A different set of issues surround the internationally low participation rate of British 16-19 year olds in vocational training. Green and Steedman (1993) identify a number of related factors:

• A system which has been - successfully - geared to high quality A levels and higher education for an elite.
• Fragmentation of responsibilities for 16-19 education and training, with over 300 bodies awarding thousands of different qualifications.
• Inadequate careers guidance on post-16 choices by comparison with, say, Germany and France.
• Lack of relatively high status vocational routes.

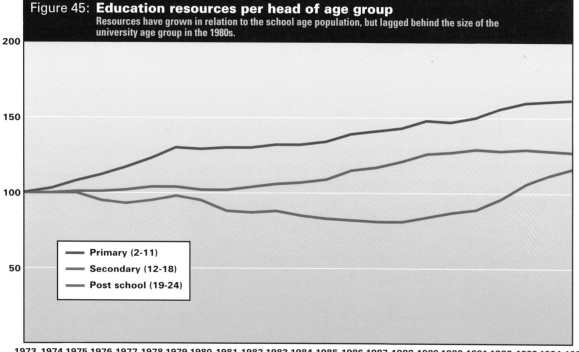

Figure 45: **Education resources per head of age group**
Resources have grown in relation to the school age population, but lagged behind the size of the university age group in the 1980s.

Source: Glennerster and Low (1990), Figure 3.5 updated

The move towards unified National Vocational Qualifications is a step forward, but Bennett, Glennerster and Nevison (1992b,c) stress that young people in Britain may have been acting entirely rationally in not taking up vocational training. In particular, investing in obtaining low level vocational qualifications (or even getting A levels without going on to higher education) may have *negative* returns. By contrast, high level vocational qualifications do add substantially to future earnings. Through the wages they offer, employers are saying they have not valued lower level vocational qualifications. Raising quality and relevance to employers turns out to be crucial.

Schools

As far as compulsory schooling is concerned, the key legislation was the 1988 Education Reform Act, parts of which introduced elements of an internal market into the sector:

• Schools were given the choice of 'opting out' from Local Education Authority (LEA) control, becoming directly 'grant-maintained'. By 1997 nearly 1,200 schools had opted out, covering 720,000 pupils.[48]

• For other schools, 'Local Management of Schools' (LMS) arrangements mean that most of the budget formerly controlled by LEAs is decentralised to school level, using formulae that depend heavily on the number of pupils.

• 'Open enrolment' is intended to give more parents the chance to send their children to their chosen school. Popular schools will then expand numbers - and with them their budgets - while unpopular ones decline.

• At the same time, part of the motivation behind the National Curriculum (the educational aspects of which raise issues going beyond the scope of this report), and its associated - and controversial - testing arrangements, is to increase the *information* going to parents.

Taken together the idea of the package is to create a system under which parents effectively have a 'voucher' for the state education of their children, with which they can shop around between local schools. Successful schools then expand, while unsuccessful ones decline, in intended analogy to other markets.

The analogy is flawed, however. Research suggests that the rational school will compete for able children, reducing not improving the educational gains for the average child.[49] Formula funding, obligations to sustain a mixed intake, and 'value added' measures of performance are all needed to make such a market fair. All are, however, technically complex to achieve.

Finally, early schooling and childcare provision remains the least developed part of British education by European standards and least well adapted to a changed labour market.[50]

Summary - key issues in education

• **Qualification levels.** At the centre of current debate is the question of whether current policies will succeed in raising the qualification levels and participation in education or training of young people in Britain to those in major competitor countries and, in particular, of how the quality and relevance of vocational qualifications can be increased, so that participation offers a better return to the trainee and employer.

• **Higher education funding.** Public resources for higher education are lagging behind rising participation. If resources per student are not to fall further, either more public spending is needed or alternative ways of funding have to be considered, such as a graduate tax or 'income contingent' loans repaid through the NIC system.

● **Competition between state schools**.
Competition between schools in the internal
market is intended to improve standards for all,
but may only do so for some at the expense of
others. If so, funding systems and regulation
arrangements may have to be adapted to offset
the problems which may otherwise emerge as
this 'market' develops.

Further reading
Learning should pay, Robert Bennett, Howard
Glennerster and Douglas Nevison (BP Educational
Service, 1992)

Departmental Report 1997, Department for
Education and Employment (HMSO, 1997)

Student Loans: Where are we now?, Nicholas Barr and
Iain Crawford (LSE Discussion Paper WSP/127, 1996)

*Into the 21st Century: An assessment of British skills
profiles and prospects*, Andy Green and Hilary
Steedman (LSE Centre for Economic Performance,
1997)

'Quasi-markets and education', Howard
Glennerster (*Economic Journal*, September 1991)

Housing

Housing conditions for most of the population are clearly better than they used to be. In 1971, there were more than 1.5 million fewer 'fit' dwellings in England and Wales than households (including 'concealed' ones); by 1991, this deficit had been reduced to about 0.3 million on comparable definitions.[51] **Figure 46** shows the extent in the improvement in general standards, with the proportion of people living without basic amenities falling from 11 to 1 per cent overall by 1990, and falling for all income groups. The numbers living at densities of one or more people per room fell from 22 to 13 per cent by 1994 and also fell in all income groups. However, those with low incomes remain much more likely to live at high densities than others and the position worsened for them in the early 1990s.

The key problem here is that despite these *general* improvements, many of the acute problems -

people living in temporary accommodation or actually out on the streets - worsened in the 1980s, while housing tenures have become much more polarised, and housing 'affordability' has become much more of a concern.

Public spending on housing

In the past the obvious feature of state housing provision in Britain was large-scale council house building. Today, Housing Benefit is the largest part of state spending on housing, and dominant issues relate to management of the existing stock of 'social' housing (councils and housing associations still owned 23 per cent of the UK stock in 1995).

Within housing spending, **Figure 47** shows the inverse relationship between current spending (mainly subsidies keeping down council rents) and Housing Benefit. As subsidies fell, rents rose

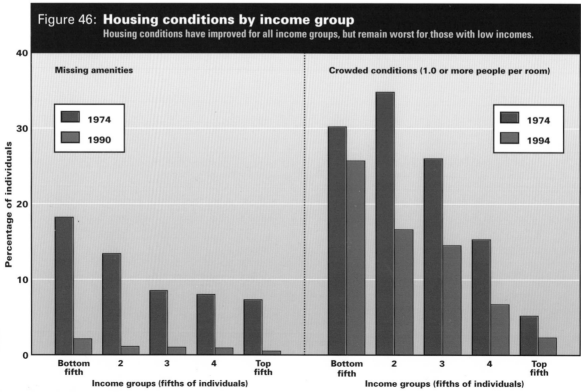

Figure 46: **Housing conditions by income group**
Housing conditions have improved for all income groups, but remain worst for those with low incomes.

Source: Hills and Mullings (1990), Tables 5.21 and 5.22 updated (based on GHS data)
Note: Individuals ranked by gross family income (allowing for family size)

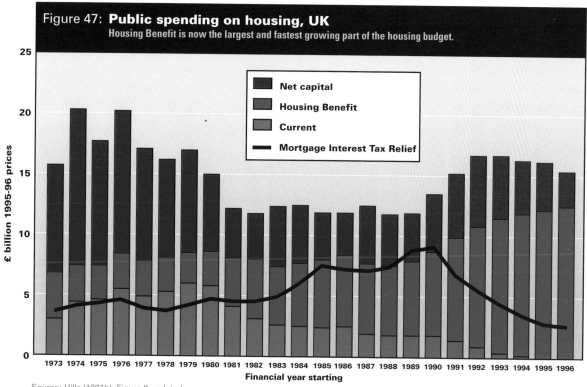

Figure 47: **Public spending on housing, UK**

Housing Benefit is now the largest and fastest growing part of the housing budget.

- Net capital
- Housing Benefit
- Current
- Mortgage Interest Tax Relief

Financial year starting

Source: Hills (1991b), Figure 8 updated

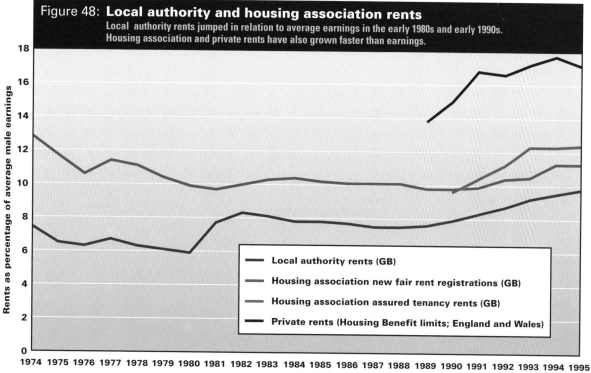

Figure 48: **Local authority and housing association rents**

Local authority rents jumped in relation to average earnings in the early 1980s and early 1990s.
Housing association and private rents have also grown faster than earnings.

- Local authority rents (GB)
- Housing association new fair rent registrations (GB)
- Housing association assured tenancy rents (GB)
- Private rents (Housing Benefit limits; England and Wales)

Financial year starting

Source: DoE (1997)

(**Figure 48**), and with them Housing Benefit paid to low income council tenants ('rent rebates'). Since 1990-91, recession, higher housing association rents (reflecting smaller *capital* grants for their new building), and higher private rents (following rent deregulation), have pushed up Housing Benefit further. By 1996-97, Housing Benefit for private and association tenants (rent allowances) was costing *more* than rebates for the much larger number of council tenants, and was increasing very rapidly.

At the same time, the cost of mortgage interest relief peaked in 1990-91, and then fell back as interest rates fell and the rate of relief was cut back to 15 per cent (with a further reduction to 10 per cent announced for 1998).

Looking at the public resources going into housing shown in Figure 47 as a whole, the total has changed little over the period. What has changed is the composition: Housing Benefit now dominates.

Rents, subsidy and affordability

Rent and subsidy policy for social housing involves two crucial trade-offs:

- Higher rents allow lower subsidy per unit, so the same amount of public spending may create more new units (if the balance of funding comes outside public spending limits).
- Higher rents extend both poverty and unemployment traps, bringing more tenants within them and making it harder for those affected to escape.

With roughly two-thirds of social tenants receiving Housing Benefit (which covers rent increases pound for pound), the long-term saving to public spending from higher rents is much less than at first sight appears, as higher future benefit payments offset lower initial capital grants. Allowing for the higher borrowing costs which housing associations face compared to government, the net saving is lower still in the case of grants to them. If the deeper poverty and unemployment traps lead to

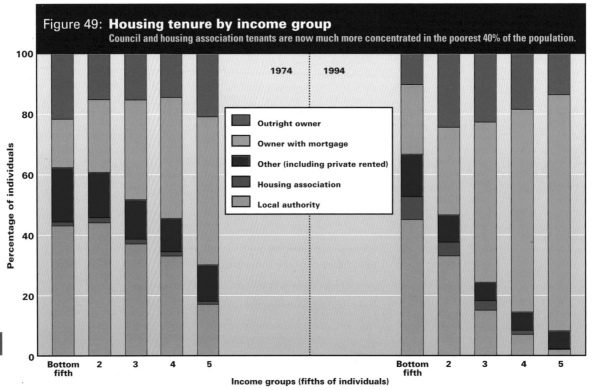

Figure 49: **Housing tenure by income group**
Council and housing association tenants are now much more concentrated in the poorest 40% of the population.

1974   1994

Outright owner
Owner with mortgage
Other (including private rented)
Housing association
Local authority

Percentage of individuals

Bottom fifth   2   3   4   5   Bottom fifth   2   3   4   5

Income groups (fifths of individuals)

Source: Hills and Mullings (1990), Tables 5.16 updated (based on GHS data)
Note: Individuals ranked by gross family income (allowing for family size)

fewer tenants taking jobs when they are available, higher rents could even increase public spending in the long run.

Polarisation and tenure change

Figure 49 compares the housing tenure of individuals by income group in 1974 and 1994. Apart from expanded owner-occupation (in all income groups except the lowest) and reduced private renting, the clearest change is the concentration of social tenants in the lowest income groups. In 1974, just under half of individuals in social housing were in the bottom 40 per cent of the income distribution. By 1994, this proportion was three-quarters. By 1995/96 only 28 per cent of heads of council tenant households in England were working, compared to 66 per cent of owner occupiers.[52]

These changes reflect the combined impact of the Right to Buy exercised by better-off tenants, the ageing of the tenant population (the proportion of individuals in council housing aged 65 and over rose from 12 to 19 per cent between 1974 and 1994[53]), the fact that access is increasingly coming through allocations under homelessness legislation, and the rising proportion of lone parents who are social tenants (63 per cent in 1989, compared to 28 per cent of all families with children).[54]

If this polarisation is accompanied by geographical segregation, it has profound social and housing management consequences. Experience with large purpose-built estates not just in Britain, but elsewhere in Europe, shows that concentrating the unemployed, single parents, teenagers, and those dependent on state benefits in particular areas not only disproportionately increases housing management and social service costs, but also makes it harder for individuals to solve their own problems.[55]

There is now concern that the combination of pressures to build larger new estates (in search of short-term cost savings) and to accept more new tenants through 'homelessness' nominations is pushing housing associations in a similar direction.[56]

Coping with such trends will not be easy, particularly as many of the social pressures come from outside housing. Allocations policies could avoid creating the worst concentrations, but housing subsidies and tax concessions in Britain reinforce pressures for those with low incomes to be tenants, those with high ones to be owners.[57] Preferences are strongly for those who can afford to do so to become owners.[58] New social housing does not have to be concentrated on large single-tenure estates, but much of the existing stock is, and will remain so. Creating the conditions where people on the worst estates can establish independent incomes goes well beyond housing policy to training and social security reform.

Who should provide social housing?

Unusually in international terms, most social housing in Britain has been owned and run by local government, with individual landlords often managing tens of thousands of units. This is beginning to change, and further change is under debate:

● Policy has been for new provision to be by housing associations, generally smaller scale than councils. But financial pressure is concentrating more development with fewer large associations, rather than many small ones.
● Some (mainly rural) councils have made 'voluntary transfers' of their stocks to newly created associations, but worries about the long-term costs of these and the finance required have led to a Treasury limit on the number allowed annually.

• The Duke of Edinburgh's Inquiry into British Housing (1991) and others have suggested transferring council housing to 'arm's-length companies'. These would be single-purpose organisations - argued to improve management - with only indirect council control. They could use the considerable equity which council housing possesses to borrow for new provision and renovation outside public spending limits - but only *if* the Treasury chose to draw the limits in that way.[59]

• The Conservative Government introduced 'Compulsory Competitive Tendering' for council housing management.[60] The idea was that councils would only continue to manage their own properties if their housing departments won competitive tenders. This was seen as a way of spurring greater efficiency and of further reducing the role of councils as 'providers' as opposed to 'purchasers' of housing services. The Labour Government is to replace this with an alternative system under which councils would not tender, but would have to show value for money.

• Initiatives like Estate Management Boards give tenants a greater say in how their estates are run, and could be spread further. As a corollary, greater tenant training would be needed.

• In countries like Germany, the private sector has provided 'social housing' in return for subsidies and eventual untied ownership. Under recent legislation, private landlords can now compete with housing associations as 'registered social landlords' for capital grants for new housing. More generally, the tax regime for private renting remains under debate. Earlier concessions under the Business Expansion Scheme (BES) led to a billion pounds of investment in private renting - but its structure encouraged letting only for four or five years, making it expensive by comparison with grants to housing associations to provide units at lower rents for thirty years or more.

• More radically, the whole idea of subsidised, 'social' housing could be abandoned altogether, with council housing departments and housing associations charging market rents and competing directly with private landlords.[61] Amongst other major consequences, with higher rents, the role of Housing Benefit would increase, raising in stronger forms the issues discussed below.

The structure of Housing Benefit

Housing Benefit was reformed in 1988 to bring its structure better into line with Income Support. However, problems remain:

• The benefit is an important contributor to the poverty trap, as it is reduced by 65 per cent of any increase in net income (with a further 20 per cent going in reduced Council Tax Benefit in most cases).

• For tenants, the payment of benefit to those in work reduces the unemployment trap, but owner-occupiers not receiving Income Support only receive normal mortgage interest relief (at 25 per cent in 1993-94, falling to 10 per cent in 1998). Some people with mortgages can be better off out of work (Figure 13).

• Like other means-tested benefits, take-up is not complete but has improved: up to 12 per cent of those entitled did not receive it in 1993-94, and up to 8 per cent of the potential benefit available was not claimed.[62]

• For recipients of even partial help, increases in rents are met pound for pound. This can lead to an 'upmarketing problem' - potential abuse by tenants or landlords taking advantage of the 'open cheque' - creating the need for controls on eligible rents and accommodation.

A range of reforms could ameliorate some of these problems:

• Given worries about the escalating cost of Housing Benefit, particularly for private rents, tighter limits on eligible rents have been brought in, with no extra benefit paid if private rents exceed the 'local reference rent'. For single people under 25 benefit is now limited to the cost of a room in shared housing. Going further, benefit could be based on less than 100 per cent of rent. However, this could mean some with very low incomes and no choice of where to live losing out, unless general compensation was built into Income Support rates. But if such compensation was high enough to protect those with high rents, there would be no overall saving, probably the reverse.

• Tapers could be cut and benefit withdrawn less quickly as income rose. But this exposes a trade-off: the poverty trap would be shallower, but would extend to higher incomes, affecting more people and extending the 'upmarketing' problem. One way round the latter difficulty would be a 'dual taper' scheme, under which higher income claimants would have the advantage of a shallower taper, but with benefit based on less than 100 per cent of rent.[63]

• In order both to counter the unemployment trap and to help counter the mortgage arrears problem which grew rapidly after 1988, Webb and Wilcox (1991) suggested a 'mortgage benefits' scheme. Under this, a proportion of mortgage interest would be eligible for Housing Benefit. The cost could be met by a relatively small cut in general mortgage interest relief. As with benefit for tenants in work, there is a trade-off: mortgage benefits would reduce the unemployment trap, but bring more into the poverty trap. The effective extension of help with the purchase of an *asset*, not just somewhere to live (as with rent rebates), would also further tilt the complicated pattern of tax and benefit advantages towards lower income owner-occupation.

The tangled nature of housing finance reflects conflicting pressures and the side-effects of other policies. While grand integrated reforms are unlikely, there are many smaller changes (going beyond the scope of this report) which could edge towards a more rational structure.[64]

Summary - key issues in housing

• **Rents and housing benefit.** A trade-off has to be struck between the greater spreading of resources enabled by higher rents for social housing and the greater dependence on means-tested Housing Benefit which results. Given associated problems like the poverty trap and potential abuse by landlords, the structure of Housing Benefit may itself require change.

• **Polarisation.** The social housing stock is increasingly occupied only by those with low incomes. This intensifies problems facing housing association and council housing managers, but also has much wider social consequences, requiring a response which goes well beyond housing policy by itself.

• **Providing social housing.** The bulk of social housing continues to be run by local authorities. Options include transferring existing stock to new organisations, such as 'arm's-length companies', or giving private landlords a role in providing new social housing.

Further reading
Inquiry into British Housing Second Report (JRF, 1991)

Thirty-nine Steps to Housing Finance Reform, John Hills (JRF, 1991)

Time for Mortgage Benefits, Steven Webb and Steve Wilcox (JRF, 1991)

Local Housing Companies: New opportunities for council housing, Steve Wilcox with Glen Bramley, Alan Ferguson, John Perry and Colin Woods (JRF, 1993)

Building for Communities, David Page (JRF, 1993)

Swimming Against the Tide: Progress and polarisation on 20 estates, Anne Power and Rebecca Tunstall (JRF, 1995)

Housing Finance Review 1997/8, Steve Wilcox (JRF, 1997)

Personal social services

The personal social services have been described as "everyone's poor relation but nobody's baby".[65] Government spending on them reached 1.3 per cent of GDP in 1995-96, making them the smallest of the welfare services examined here. They are also the area where government probably plays the smallest role in total provision. In particular, more than six million adults provide informal care to elderly or disabled relatives and others. Estimates of the 'money value' of such care range from roughly the same as Government spending to four times as large.[66]

Many of the key issues facing social workers and the voluntary agencies - like child abuse and coping with family breakdown - go beyond the scope of this report. Three elements of the current debate are discussed below:

(a) The introduction of a 'purchaser/provider split' into social services;
(b) The scope for older people to pay for their own care; and
(c) The position of informal carers.

(a) The purchaser/provider split

Since April 1993, local authority social service departments (SSDs) have been working in a new way, emphasising their role as 'purchasers' of care on behalf of their clients, rather than as direct 'providers' of, say, residential homes for elderly people.

This change, legislated in 1990, goes back to the Griffiths Report of 1988, and the subsequent White Paper, *Caring for People*.[67] It is also a reaction to the huge growth in the amounts which were being paid through the social security budget - as 'board and lodging' payments through SB/IS - for residential care,

from £10 million in 1979 to £1.2 billion in 1990.[68] The equivalent of this budget has now been transferred to local authorities.

At the heart of the reforms is the idea that each SSD appoints a 'care manager' for each client. This care manager then uses the department's budget to purchase from outside an appropriate 'package' of care on the client's behalf. This is intended to secure the following advantages:

• Previously, much of the funding was tied (through social security) to spending on residential care. Now the same resources could be used in a more appropriate way, for instance to provide support for those who could then remain at home.
• As with other areas of 'quasi-market' welfare reform, the new arrangements are intended to create competition between a range of potential providers, with resulting efficiency gains.

Glennerster and Lewis (1996), reviewing the introduction of the new scheme, found that it was driven far more by the need to put a cap on government spending (previously open-ended under DSS payments) than by the advantages of a more flexible use of funds. More generally:

• The potential for productive 'resource switching' was, in fact, limited. Most of the budget transferred to SSDs in April 1993 was already committed, and where it could be switched, it was suggested that at most 17 per cent of residents were inappropriately in residential care.[69]
• In some respects, the changes *reduced* people's direct choices: previously they could choose a residential home themselves using social security money. Now such choices will be exercised on

their behalf by a care manager. People must now become a social services 'client' to gain access to public funding, something they might rather avoid.

- Reorganisation and the new 'quasi-market' structure may add to costs, and it is not clear how much competition amongst providers will eventually emerge. Le Grand concluded:

> *"If indeed cost containment was the principal motivation for the initiators of reforms, then they have probably made a serious mistake."*[70]

- There is no national policy to even out resources over the country in relation to needs: people in the same position in different areas will be treated unequally.

(b) Personal sources of funding for care

Whilst the growth in the elderly population as a whole may have slowed, the very elderly population is growing more rapidly: over-85s are projected to rise from 1.6 per cent of the population in 1991 to 3.8 per cent in 2041 (Figure 21). This growth puts pressures on several parts of the welfare state. One reaction has been what appears like passing the parcel as the NHS saves costs by closing down long-stay geriatric wards, shifting to social security funding of residential care, which has been passed in turn to local authorities.

A second reaction is to examine the scope for people to fund their own care when it is needed. Oldman (1991) has reviewed possible alternatives to state funding:

- Payment out of the current 'surplus income' of those needing care. Oldman estimates that only about 10 per cent of those over 70 could afford to do so.
- Running down financial savings. Given the capital rules for social security, this is how many people pay for the first few months of residential care already.

- Use of 'home equity' - converting the assets people, who may not have high incomes, own in the form of housing into a regular income stream. However, research suggests that the scope for this is fairly limited, particularly after falls in interest rates and house prices. **Figure 50** shows that only 6 per cent of households with a head aged 65 or more fall into the 'house rich - income poor' group for whom this is a solution. Even where people do, the potential scale of income from 'equity release schemes' - around £25 per week - is very small by comparison with care costs.
- Earlier planning for old age and insurance against potential care costs. However, US experience is not promising: fourteen years after Long Term Care insurance was launched there, it was covering less than 1 per cent of all long term care, and,

> *"Uncertainties about future costs and how to assess risks have resulted in [insurance] policies that are long in limitations and short on full protection."*[71]

An examination of the private insurance policies available in the UK in 1996 found similarly that tight conditions were set for potential claims under them, requiring high levels of disability for someone to be eligible.[72] Policy costs looked high in relation to the risks people face based on current rates of usage of residential care. However, given uncertainty about people's requirements in twenty or thirty years' time it is very hard to evaluate the value for money given by such policies. 'Market failure' problems for this kind of insurance are particularly severe.

- As an alternative, the Joseph Rowntree Foundation's *Inquiry into Meeting the Costs of Continuing Care* (1996) suggested a universal compulsory national care insurance scheme, with people paying into the scheme in relation to their incomes (as under social insurance), but with the scheme run by a National Care Corporation at arm's-length from the public sector.

(c) Informal carers

The proportion of adults reporting that they were caring for someone who was 'sick, handicapped or elderly' rose from 14 to 16 per cent between 1985 and 1990.[73] Both their circumstances and caring responsibilities vary widely. In particular, those caring for someone within the same household and those spending more than 20 hours per week on such activities (each about 4 per cent of adults, with some overlap) have lower incomes, lower employment rates, and lower earnings when at work than non-carers. This not only affects their current standard of living, but may well reduce their future pension rights.

The social security system recognises this situation in two ways:
• Those spending more than 35 hours per week looking after someone who is themselves entitled to Attendance Allowance or equivalent benefits (that is, severely disabled) can claim Invalid Care Allowance. In 1990 one-third of those caring for someone in the same household or caring for more than 20 hours per week said they were receiving ICA.[74] The numbers receiving ICA have since more than doubled,[75] but a proportion of the two vulnerable groups are still ineligible. When benefit is received, it is not high - £37.35 per week in 1997-98 - and it is deducted when other means-tested benefits are assessed, so its net effect is often small, certainly much smaller than typical earnings foregone.
• Home Responsibility Protection 'credits' towards the basic pension and SERPS are given to those who meet the same criteria as ICA, but again this is a minority of those whose lifetime earnings and pension rights are affected by informal care.

Summary - key issues in personal social services

• **The purchaser/provider split.** Social service departments have been given new responsibilities as 'purchasers' of care on their clients' behalf, leading to questions of whether

Figure 50: Incomes and housing equity
Relatively few elderly people households currently fit the description 'house rich/income poor'.

'House rich/income poor'

High housing equity
Low/medium housing equity
No housing equity

Notes: 1 Low income is less than £75 per week for single person or less than £150 per week for a couple
2 High housing equity is greater than £40,000 for a single person or greater than £60,000 for a couple
3 Figures adapted to 1993 prices

Low income (58%)   High income (42%)

Source: Gibbs (1993)

the main effect of the reform has been to cap government spending rather than give more flexibility in the services available to beneficiaries, and whether they reduce the choice which users can exercise directly.

• **Personal funding for long-term care.** There are proposals for more use of personal resources such as savings, home equity or private long-term care insurance plans as an addition to or partial substitute for public funding, but evidence suggests limited scope for doing so. Alternatively, there are proposals for a compulsory national care insurance scheme, run either through national insurance or at arm's length from the public sector.

• **Informal carers.** Benefits like Invalid Care Allowance and national insurance credits could be extended to compensate those with the greatest responsibilities for informal care.

Further reading
Quasi-markets and community care, Julian Le Grand (School of Advanced Urban Studies, Bristol, 1993)

Paying for Care: Personal sources of funding care, Christine Oldman (JRF, 1991)

Housing Wealth in Later Life: A mixed blessing, Ian Gibbs (Centre for Housing Policy, University of York, 1993)

'Challenging the Invisibility of Carers: Mapping informal care nationally', Maria Evandrou (in F. Laczko and C. Victor (eds) *Social Policy and Older People*, Gower, 1992)

Implementing the New Community Care, Jane Lewis and Howard Glennerster (Open University Press, 1996)

Report of the JRF Inquiry into meeting the costs of continuing care (JRF, 1996)

Private Welfare Insurance and Social Security: Pushing the boundaries, Tania Burchardt and John Hills (JRF, 1997)

3

Conclusion

Although the second part of this report was divided along the conventional lines of government department responsibilities, it will have been evident that related themes recur throughout the different services. This concluding section reviews these cross-cutting issues. In particular, in contrast to much of the current debate which starts from the assumption that policy is boxed in by fiscal constraints, it highlights the wide range of inter-related options which face welfare policy.

These options, and the different dimensions in which choices can be made, are summarised in **Figure 51**. This places different policy instruments and options in approximate order across four main dimensions, running from left to right across the diagram (and, to a certain extent, politically). Associated with each of these main dimensions is a 'subsidiary dimension' (running up and down the diagram) in which policies can vary.

Thus, in the first layer of the figure, options which increase welfare spending as a share of national income are towards the left, with those which do so incrementally, rather than as a 'step' change, towards the top left. The second layer has policies placing more emphasis on means-testing as a way of targeting on the right and those with least link to individual circumstances, as opposed to income, towards the top right. The third layer presents options for financing welfare provision, with finance most linked to a particular service on the right, and systems with the strongest links to individual use or rights to services towards the bottom. Finally, the fourth layer presents options for welfare provision, with centralised public providers on the left, and options which give stronger control to service users towards the bottom.

While these choices are to a certain extent inter-related, there is no constraint which forces decisions to move in similar directions in the different dimensions, nor any presumption that the same direction for change will be appropriate for all services.

The scale of welfare spending

Much current discussion about the welfare state starts from the presumption that a 'demographic time bomb' is ticking away which will cause an unsustainable explosion of welfare costs unless action is taken to defuse it by cutting back now.

It is clear that such concerns have been considerably exaggerated. There are upward pressures on welfare spending for a whole range of reasons, including ageing of the population, the maturing of SERPS, worries about educational standards compared to other countries, and caring for very elderly people. However, looking over several decades, the total of such pressures is no greater than the effects of recession and electoral cycles on welfare spending over the three years from 1989. The future performance of the economy, and the level of unemployment in particular, will have as great an effect as demography by itself.

The implication of this is that Britain has a real *choice* about the future of the welfare state, indeed a series of choices, rather than one particular route being inevitable. It would, of course, be easier if economic performance improved, if resources could be transferred from other areas of government spending, or if borrowing were to rise from its current (historically high) level. In the absence of these escape routes, there is, however, a fundamental choice:

• We could, as a nation, decide to maintain or even improve welfare services in relation to particular needs, including maintaining the *relative* values of cash benefits and pay of workers in the welfare services like nurses, doctors and teachers. To do this would mean that welfare spending would rise slowly as a percentage of national income, and with it the overall level of taxation. However, the rise implied by maintaining services as the population ages over the next fifty years would not take Britain's welfare spending above the share of national income already spent in most other European countries, which face much greater future demographic pressures. There is nothing inherently infeasible about this choice.

● Alternatively, it could be decided that the limits of acceptable levels of taxation to finance welfare services have already been reached. This implies that public welfare services would have to become less generous in relation to contemporary living standards or to certain needs than they are now. It is current policy that this should happen incrementally through price-linking rather than through linking benefit levels to income. However, this is not the only way in which the aim could be achieved - relative benefit values could be maintained, but entitlement restricted to a smaller group, for instance by raising pension ages or concentrating Child Benefit on younger children.

Independently of this fundamental choice, the social and economic environment in which the welfare state operates has changed substantially since many of its institutions were set in place or remodelled after the Second World War. At present, family structures and the labour market are changing rapidly, and the distribution of incomes which people receive from the market became much more unequal during the 1980s. It is inevitable that institutions across the welfare state should be under scrutiny in the face of such changes. Both the form of and

balance between services may have to adapt, so it is hardly surprising that the wide range of options reviewed in Part 2 and summarised in Figure 51 (itself only a limited selection) is currently under discussion. Just as it is not inevitable that the welfare state has to be scaled back, so there is no compulsion to move in the same direction on all fronts: expansion may be appropriate in one area, retrenchment in another.

Ways of targeting welfare

The aims of the welfare state go well beyond the narrow objective of relieving poverty or simply redistributing income from rich to poor. In its wider roles - such as smoothing out income over the life cycle, insuring all against common risks, redistributing from men to women - it is clearly successful, although the appropriate scale of such activities is a matter of debate.

None the less, the welfare state as currently constructed *is* 'targeted' on those with lower incomes. With the probable exception of higher education spending on students who live away from home, the value of benefits and services going to those with lower incomes is greater than the taxes which they pay to finance them (under any plausible allocation of financing costs). The reverse is true for higher income groups. For cash benefits, the National Health Service and compulsory state schooling, the *absolute* value going to those with low incomes is greater than that going to those with high incomes, even before one looks at the net position after allowing for financing.

The targeting debate is not therefore over *whether* to target, but about *how* to target. A wide variety of instruments are available, most already in use in one form or another:

Figure 51: A welfare state policy options map

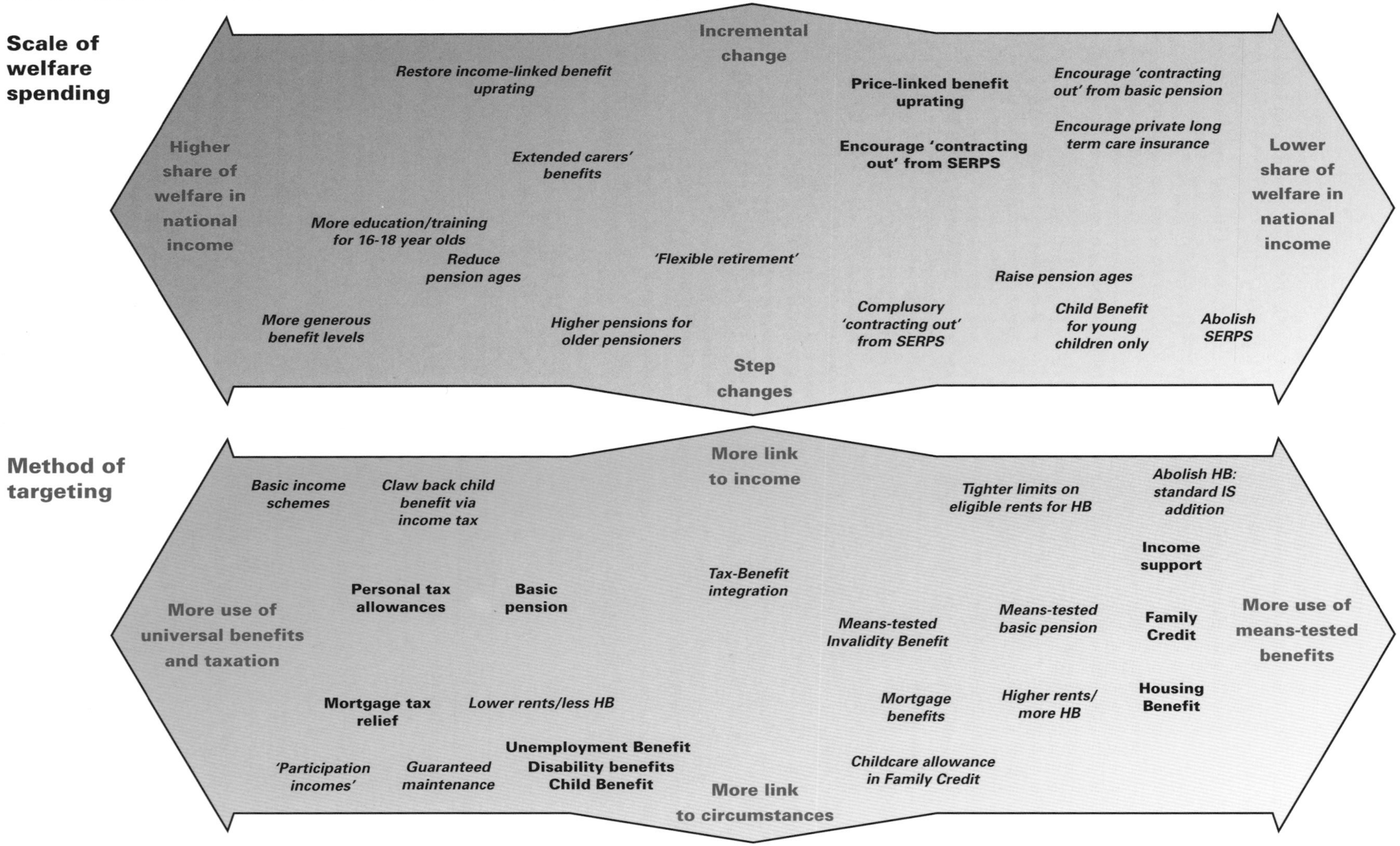

Scale of welfare spending

Method of targeting

Source of public finance

Less link to individual use

Finance linked to service

Hypothecated taxes

NHS Tax

National Care Insurance Scheme

Charges for GP visits/'hotel charges' for hospitals

Student loans

Prescription charges

Retain social security tax without contribution conditions on benefits

Graduate tax/income contingent loans

National Insurance contributions

SERPS rights

Minimum state pension

More link to individual use

Merge income tax and NICs

Funding from general taxation

Finance for general purposes

System of provision

Greater provider/purchaser control

Private provision/competition

Private landlord provision of social housing

'Voucher' systems

Compulsory competitive tendering for council housing management

Private Sector Leasing (housing)

PSS 'care managers'

'Voluntary transfers' of council housing

Housing associations

Friendly societies

'Arms length' housing companies

Tenant ownership co-operatives

GP fundholders

Hospital trusts

Opted out schools

Greater user control

District Health Authorities

Ordinary GP budgets

Council housing

LEA Schools

Local Management of schools

Estate Management Boards

Public provision/planning

Note: Policy instruments in bold already in use; those in italics are options for introduction or expansion.

Conclusion

- Provision according to needs or contingencies which disproportionately affect those with lower incomes;
- 'Universal' coverage of contingencies which affect all income groups, but with flat-rate benefits financed by taxes or contributions which rise with income.
- Means-testing, with those whose incomes exceed a threshold excluded from coverage or asked to make a contribution.
- Use of the tax system to give flat-rate tax-free allowances to those with particular needs, or to clawback benefits from those with higher incomes.

Proposals reviewed above include alternative ways of using these instruments, but one factor remains inescapable. If those with low incomes receive a net benefit from a service and its financing while those with higher incomes make net contributions, then, at some point in between, *net* incomes cannot rise as fast as *market* incomes. The choices come as to *where* this withdrawal takes place and what *form* any implied disincentives will take. It may be an 'unemployment trap', as can result from the treatment of mortgage interest by social security. Or it may a 'poverty trap', as affects families with low earnings. Or the withdrawal may be spread out over a wide income range, as with 'universal' tax-financed benefits. The problem of designing targeting mechanisms is one of trying to ensure that the adverse incentives are at levels and in places where they do least damage.

Paying for welfare
A further series of choices comes in the form in which public finance for welfare is raised. Again, most of the potential instruments are already in use in one form or another:

- Use of general taxation and public borrowing, unrelated to the individual service.

- Use of 'hypothecated taxes', where the money raised is earmarked for a particular form of spending.
- Use of contributions, where the amount an individual pays has an effect on benefits received later (such contributions need not necessarily be earmarked for paying for that service).
- Recovering part of the cost of provision through charges which bear more heavily on those making greater use of particular services.
- Recovering the cost of provision from its beneficiaries at a later date, for instance, through some form of loan system.

The bulk of British welfare spending has been traditionally financed through the first route, but all of the others are in use, ranging from National Insurance Contributions to rents for council housing, prescription charges and student loans. The mix is not, however, inevitable - hence proposals discussed above for expanding the use of hypothecated taxes, others for reducing their use (through merging income tax and national insurance), for widening the range of services for which the NHS makes charges, or for reforming student finance to recover costs through 'income contingent loans' or graduate taxes.

In making this choice, scope for potential improvement on current arrangements may be indicated by an apparent paradox. When people are surveyed about the choice between better public services and higher taxation on the one hand, and reduced services and lower taxation on the other, an increasing majority opts for the former. On the other hand, surveys and voting behaviour suggest that people may not trust politicians to spend any higher taxes in the way they would like. This suggests a possible case for more reliance on instruments other than general taxation.

But again, there are trade-offs. Hypothecated financing may result in some services doing well from buoyant revenue sources while others suffer, rather than over-arching decisions being taken as to which service needs the next pound most or can absorb a cut least painfully. Charging more to the direct users of services in one way or another may be inequitable - as it is those in greatest need who use them - or it may create disincentives to use a service, even if doing so would result in wider social benefits (as with education and training).

The system of provision

Since the War, the British welfare state has mostly taken the form of publicly financed services provided and run by large-scale public institutions - the NHS, state schools, and council housing. Again, there is nothing inevitable about this. Public *finance* can just as easily be channelled through private or voluntary providers as through public ones. Where there are public providers, they do not have to be single national institutions.

It is here rather than in the overall scale of the welfare state that there is currently most rapid change. Through a series of reforms, particularly in the late 1980s, the Conservative Government separated out the roles of 'purchaser' and 'provider'. In the NHS this involves some GPs making more choices over the allocation of the resources their patients use and hospital trusts competing with one another to win contracts from GPs and District Health Authorities. In housing, it involves councils retaining their responsibilities to find homes for those classified as homeless, but not necessarily doing so from council housing - using housing associations or private sector leasing arrangements instead. In education, budgets have been devolved to schools, and open enrolment and funding formulae are intended to make schools compete

with one another for pupils. In the personal social services, local authorities are appointing 'care managers' who purchase 'care packages' from outside on their clients' behalf, rather than the local authority running its own residential homes, for instance.

The aims of these reforms are similar - devolution of resource allocation decisions to smaller scale organisations, and the promotion of competition between providers. Both are intended to produce greater efficiency in the use of existing resources and thereby to result in better services or to restrain growth in costs.

The jury is still out on the effects of these changes - and it may well return different verdicts for particular services. The evidence so far suggests that some of the hoped-for gains are being realised. But there are other effects. First, the new 'internal markets' themselves use resources to establish and run, which may offset efficiency gains. There may also be efficiency losses from unco-ordinated decision-making.

Second, while there may be those who benefit from their access to a successful 'provider' - GP, school, or housing association - this may come at the expense of others whose agents are less successful in winning resources on their behalf in the internal market-place.

Third, the reforms do not allow central government to escape the problem of establishing formulae by which the publicly raised finance is distributed between the individual providers. It is very hard to establish funding formulae which do not leave opportunities for 'cream-skimming' - providers spotting how to make sure that their caseload is weighted towards those patients, pupils or clients whose particular costs are likely to be lower than allowed for in the formula.

83

Conclusion

Finally, there is the question of who exercises the choices: is it really the users of the service or is it someone acting on their behalf - do the reforms 'empower' the users or the professional purchasers?

As well as changes in the organisation of what remain public providers, there could also be changes in the balance of Britain's 'mixed economy' of welfare ranging from the tax-financed NHS, through welfare organisations supported by voluntary donations, friendly societies, employer and personal pension schemes, to unpaid informal care by individuals for their relatives and neighbours.

The mixture is not entirely accidental. Whilst the private sector is the most efficient solution in some areas, it manifestly is not in others - health care in the USA being a stark example. It is not just that public involvement in some form is necessary where the effect of the system is to transfer incomes from rich to poor or to those whose needs exceed their resources. There are other areas - probably accounting for the bulk of the welfare state's activities - where people are at one time paying for services which they themselves receive at another. The state is involved here because, left to itself, the market would not produce an efficient solution. 'Risk-pooling' across the community can give a better deal to the ordinary person than private insurance schemes whose terms have to be geared to the 'bad risks'. State involvement in education and training can lead to a more productive economy than leaving it to individual employers, who may not themselves accrue the benefits from training potentially mobile employees.

On the other hand, there are areas where state provision, or at least the particular form it takes, may get *in the way* of private provision. As an example, Beveridge's ideal for state pensions was that they should provide an underpinning on which people would build additional private sector rights. But, for pensioners receiving means-tested benefits and caught in the 'savings trap', there is little point in making - or having made - additional private provision. In such cases attempts to promote the role of the private sector through 'targeting' may have entirely perverse effects. As more people are affected by means-testing, so such problems grow.

Beyond welfare

Parts of the welfare state represent a success story of organising provision for inescapable needs like health care or education. But the fact that more than one in six of the population is dependent on the state safety net, Income Support, does not represent a triumph of welfare provision, rather that the welfare state is having to pick up the pieces of failure elsewhere in the economy.

Macro-economic policy, investment, training, creation of new enterprises, regeneration of declining regions, ensuring that everyone can work to their full potential, coping with the consequences of family change and family breakdown, and changing the dynamics of communities where children are growing up without seeing the prospect of a job or of control over their own lives, all lie beyond the scope of this report - but they are probably what are most critical for the future of welfare.

Notes

Part 1

1 See HM Treasury 1997, Tables 3.1-3.5 for details of the information in this sub-section.

2 DSS, 1993b, p. 2.

3 On OECD definitions. By comparison with the British welfare spending figures above, general housing spending is excluded, but spending on 'active labour market policies' and some other items is included. UK figures are based on UK sources for social security spending.

4 Ermisch (1990) similarly suggests that ageing by itself from 1991 to 2026 would add only 10 per cent to per capita spending on health and personal social services. The age distribution of health spending used here is the "high variation" case from Hills (1992), with updated spending and population estimates; assuming less variation in spending with age would reduce estimated growth.

5 Willetts (1993) reaches similar conclusions.

6 Support ratios are an imperfect guide to the effect of ageing on taxpayers, as they neglect changing employment patterns, the effects of changing school-age populations, and taxes paid by elderly people (see Falkingham, 1989).

7 Assuming that GDP per capita grows in line with the assumed annual earnings growth of 1.5 per cent.

8 See Berthoud (1993).

9 For some purposes Housing Benefit should be excluded. This is because, although its cost has risen, a major reason for this was *reductions* in subsidies to council and housing association tenants, which implied offsetting savings to other parts of Government. It is therefore better to look at Housing Benefit and other housing spending together, as is done in Part 2.

10 See Barr (1992) for a review.

11 The second to tenth decile groups each paid between 34 and 38 per cent of their gross incomes in tax in 1995-96. The bottom group paid 51 per cent of their gross income in tax. This counts Council Tax rebates as part of gross income, however, and gross payments as a tax. If one counts *net* payments as a tax, the bottom tenth still paid at least 45 per cent of their gross income (excluding rebates) in tax, *more* than the other income groups.

12 The benefits in cash and kind allowed for here averaged £6,621 per household; taxes averaged £7,635.

13 For more details and further explanation, see Falkingham, Hills and Lessof (1993) or Falkingham and Hills (1995).

14 Thus, for instance, the results show the effects on individual pension rights of complete working lives under the rules of the State Earnings Related Pension Scheme as they applied for new entrants in 1991.

15 Unlike the cross-sectional results in Figure 10, 'final' income here does not allow for indirect taxes, housing benefits or local taxes.

16 The lifetime tax payments allowed for here are scaled exactly to cover the costs of the welfare services.

17 These results assume that welfare services are financed by a share of the whole tax system, in effect by a percentage of gross income. If it was assumed that they were paid for only by *direct* taxes, the 'savings bank' share would fall to two-thirds, and the 'Robin Hood' share would rise to one-third.

18 See Falkingham and Hills (1995), chapter 3.

19 See Atkinson (1987) and Barr (1992) for surveys of much of this literature.

20 DSS (1997), Figure 32.

21 DSS (1997), Table 7.

22 Blundell (1992) gives a survey of the evidence.

23 Atkinson and Micklewright (1989) identified 38 ways in which its rules were changed between 1979 and 1988, 33 of which reduced entitlement. In addition, the replacement of Unemployment Benefit by JSA reduced the maximum period before means-testing to 6 months from one year.

24 Derived from OPCS (1993a), Table 5.31. Figures are for married women aged 16-59 with husbands under 65.

25 Irwin and Morris (1993).

26 See Marmor *et al.* (1990), pp. 104-114 and references given there for opposing views.

27 Marsh and McKay (1993), pp. 139 and 186.

28 OPCS (1993a), Table 5.14.

29 Roll (1992b) quoted in Holtermann (1993).

30 Holtermann (1993), p.44.

31 See Atkinson (1991a, 1992) for a detailed discussion.

32 See Waldfogel (1993) for an analysis.

33 See Bennett, Glennerster and Nevison (1992a,b and c) for an analysis of the private returns to different kinds of education.

34 Quoted by Harris (1994).

35 The recent debate started with what seemed to be powerful evidence for a negative effect in the US case in Feldstein (1974), but subsequent research has cast doubt on the findings (Barr 1992, pp. 773-4).

36 Assuming that capital is generating a gross return of 5 per cent. This situation arises because of the way the capital income is treated for means-tested benefits.

37 Beveridge (1942), p.164.

38 Much of the information in this section is taken from Kiernan and Wicks (1990) and Kiernan and Estaugh (1993).

39 DSS (1996a), Table D1, after housing costs.

40 Evandrou (1992).

41 See Roll (1992a) for a discussion of the problems of measuring poverty.

42 Income after housing costs may be more appropriate than the 'before housing costs' (BHC) series as a measure of trends in incomes when real rents have risen substantially, adding to the Housing Benefit of those receiving it and hence their BHC incomes, but not their living standards.

43 There is some controversy over the effects on this figure of misreporting of incomes by the self-employed. If the self-employed are excluded from the picture, the fall for the bottom tenth is 6 per cent.

44 Figures are for the medians of each decile group (tenth) of population. For detailed discussion of the position up to the early 1990s, see Hills (1995 and 1996).

45 Lines are not shown for shares of post-tax income, as these followed almost exactly the same course as gross incomes.

Part 2

1 DSS (1997), Table 1 and Figure 23; HM Treasury (1997), Table 3.5.

2 See Burchardt and Hills (1997) for detailed discussion of the economic problems of private insurance for risks now covered by 'social insurance'.

3 See Le Grand (1995) for a discussion of the philosophical issues involved in why society provides such protection.

4 DSS (1996a), Table B4.

5 See Parker and Sutherland (1991) for a detailed examination of the case of Child Benefit.

6 DSS (1997), Figure 12.

7 The most fully worked-out proposals for tax-benefit integration in Britain remain those of Dilnot, Kay and Morris (1984). For further discussion of some of the issues involved, see Hills (1988) and Meadows (1997).

8 See, for instance, Parker (1989) or the publications of the group *Citizens Income*. For a discussion of 'partial basic incomes', see Parker and Sutherland (1991).

9 Atkinson (1989), Chapter 16 and Parker (1989).

10 Atkinson and Micklewright (1989).

11 Glennerster and Evans (1994).

12 Mulgan and Murray (1993).

13 DSS (1993a), p. 10.

14 Atkinson (1991a, 1993).

15 See Roll (1991) for an examination of the wide variety of definitions of the 'benefit family'.

16 Veit-Wilson (1994). Glennerster and Evans (1994) and Atkinson (1991b).

17 Bradshaw (1993), Table 7.2.

18 Marsh and McKay (1993), Table 9.1. Indicators included items like two or more problem debts, or saying "always worried about money" *and* "in deep financial trouble".

19 See Berthoud (1993) for an analysis of the growth of Invalidity Benefit. He concludes that over half of the growth has been due to demographic change or to substitution for the basic pension. The rest is not due to a greater *inflow* of new claimants, but rather a slower *outflow*, as jobs have become harder to find, particularly for disabled people.

20 Abel-Smith (1994).

21 Statistics in this sub-section based on DSS (1991).

22 The change will be phased in between 2010 and 2020, so that women born before 1950 are unaffected, but those born from 1954 receive pensions at 65.

23 Assuming a common pension age of 63.

24 The net cost allows for offsetting savings in Income Support and extra tax revenue which higher SERPS and increased basic pension entitlement would generate. If the *gross* cost was funded *only* by NICs, which are charged on less than half of national income, the combined contribution rate would have to rise by 7.2 percentage points by 2030 (Government Actuary, 1995, Table 11).

25 The maximum results from the Upper Earnings Limit for relevant earnings, assumed to remain at 7.5 times the basic pension.

26 OPCS (1993a), Table 6.26.

27 See the Labour Party's Commission on Social Justice (1994) and Field and Owen (1993) for proposals of this kind.

28 Although the analysis in Hills (1992) suggests that this is not the case in Britain if one looks at the welfare state as a whole.

29 Hills (1989), Table 5.

30 Department of Health (1997).

31 Robinson and Le Grand (1994) and Glennerster, Matsaganis and Owens (1994).

32 These projections assume that as people live longer they still require as much treatment at a given age as before. It could be that they also stay healthier longer, and increased spending needs are delayed. If so, such indices overstate the effect of ageing.

33 Figures from the Public Finance Foundation. Given the rising average skill level of NHS workers, and the way in which settlements have been tilted towards the lower paid, these comparisons may *understate* the extent to which NHS pay has fallen behind comparators in the private sector.

34 Barney Hayhoe, MP, quoted by Le Grand, Winter and Woolley (1990).

35 Department of Health (1997). Part of the fall after 1989-90 reflects changes in accounting procedures by NHS Trusts.

36 See Mulgan and Murray (1993) for a proposition of this kind. However, the Labour Party's Commission on Social Justice (1994) objected to an NHS tax on the grounds that it would make it too easy for NHS resources to be increased, even if other spending was more urgent.

37 Based here on equivalent gross income.

38 Evandrou, Falkingham, Le Grand and Winter (1992).

39 Townsend and Davidson (1982); Whitehead (1987); Illsley and Le Grand (1987); Wilkinson (1996).

40 Le Grand, Winter and Woolley (1990), Table 4.15.

41 Dorling (1997), Tables 14 and 16. See Wilkinson (1996) for a general discussion of health inequalities.

42 See Glennerster and Low (1990) for a discussion.

43 Department for Education and Employment (1997), Table 4.1 and Figure 4.2. The A level figures are for those obtained by full-time study only.

44 Glennerster and Low (1990), Table 3.14 updated.

45 Figures from Public Finance Foundation. Again, overall averages conceal composition changes which affect the position of particular teaching grades, for example, relative to private sector comparators.

46 Department for Education and Employment (1996), Figure 13.

47 DfEE (1997), Table 1.13.

48 Department for Education and Employment (1997), p. 73.

49 Glennerster (1991).

50 Hewitt (1993); House of Commons Education Committee (1989).

51 Hills and Mullings (1990), Table 5.11 updated using DoE (1993b). On the current, more stringent, definition of 'fitness', the deficit rises to over one million.

52 DoE (1997), Table 12.13.

53 ONS (1997b).

54 Bradshaw and Millar (1991).

55 Power (1993 and 1997).

56 Page (1993).

57 Hills (1991a).

58 Saunders (1990).

59 See Wilcox *et al.* (1993) for an analysis of the proposal. The problem with getting borrowing by such organisations outside public spending controls relates to whether the councils are effectively guaranteeing it. If so, it all counts as public spending (although in logic, only the actuarial value of the risk involved should do so).

60 DoE (1992a).

61 See, for instance, Coleman (1989).

62 DSS (1996b), Table H4.03.

63 See Hills (1991a, b) for a description.

64 See Hills (1991b) for an evaluation of some of these.

65 Evandrou *et al* (1990).

66 Oldman (1991) quotes a Laing and Buisson estimate of £5 billion per year (valuing carers' time at £2.50 per hour). Evandrou *et al.* (1990) quote an FPSC estimate for 1987 of between £15-24 billion (at £4.09 per hour). The JRF Inquiry into *Meeting the costs of continuing care* (1996) quotes an estimate of £35 billion (at £7 per hour).

67 Department of Health (1989).

68 Oldman (1991), p.4.

69 Schorr (1992), p.21.

70 Le Grand (1993), p.11.

71 M. Moon writing in the *Journal of the American Geriatrics Society* quoted by Oldman (1991), p.26.

72 Burchardt and Hills (1997).

73 Evandrou (1992, 1993), based on GHS data.

74 Evandrou (1993), Table 8.

75 DSS (1993a), Table 6.

Bibliography

Abel-Smith, B (1994), 'The Beveridge Report: Its origins and outcomes', in Hills, Ditch and Glennerster (1994).

Atkinson, A B (1987), 'Income maintenance and social insurance: A survey', in Auerbach, A and M Feldstein (eds.), *Handbook of Public Economics*, vol.II. Amsterdam: Elsevier Science Publishers.

Atkinson, A B (1989), *Poverty and Social Security*. Hemel Hempstead: Harvester Wheatsheaf.

Atkinson, A B (1991a), 'Social insurance', *Geneva Papers on Risk and Social Insurance Theory*, 16(2), 113-131.

Atkinson, A B (1991b), 'A national minimum? A history of ambiguity in the determination of benefit scales in Britain', in T and D Wilson (eds.), *The State and Social Welfare*. London: Longman.

Atkinson, A B (1992), 'Institutional features of unemployment insurance and the working of the labour market', in P Dasgupta, D Gale, O Hart and E Maskin (eds.), *Economic Analysis of Markets and Games*. Cambridge, Mass.: MIT Press.

Atkinson, A B (1993), 'Beveridge, the national minimum, and its future in a European context', Welfare State Programme Discussion Paper WSP/85. London: London School of Economics.

Atkinson, A B and Micklewright, J (1989), 'Turning the screw: Benefits for the unemployed, 1979-1988', in Atkinson (1989).

Atkinson, A B and Sutherland, H (1992), 'Two nations in early retirement? The case of Britain', in A B Atkinson and M Rein (eds.), *Age, Work and Social Security*. London: Macmillan.

Baldwin, S and Falkingham, J (1994), *Social Insurance and Social Change: New challenges to the Beveridge model*. Hemel Hempstead: Harvester Wheatsheaf.

Barr, N (1988), 'The mirage of private unemployment insurance', Welfare State Programme Discussion Paper WSP/34. London: London School of Economics.

Barr, N (1989), 'Social insurance as an efficiency device', *Journal of Public Policy*, 9(1), 59-82.

Barr, N (1992), 'Economic theory and the welfare state: A survey and reinterpretation', *Journal of Economic Literature*, 30, 741-803.

Barr, N (1993), *The Economics of the Welfare State* (new edition). London: Weidenfeld and Nicholson.

Barr, N and Coulter, F (1990), 'Social security: Problem or solution?', in Hills (1990).

Barr, N and Falkingham, J (1993), 'Paying for learning', Welfare State Programme Discussion Paper WSP/94. London: London School of Economics.

Bennett, R, Glennerster, H and Nevison, D (1992a), 'Investing in skill: To stay on or not to stay on?', *Oxford Review of Economic Policy*, 8(2).

Bennett, R, Glennerster, H and Nevison, D (1992b), *Learning should Pay*. Poole: BP Education.

Bennett, R, Glennerster, H and Nevison, D (1992c), 'Investing in skill: Expected returns to vocational training', Welfare State Programme Discussion Paper WSP/83. London: London School of Economics.

Berthoud, R (1993), *Invalidity Benefit: Where will the savings come from?* London: Policy Studies Institute.

Beveridge, W H (1942), *Social Insurance and Allied Services*, Cmd. 6404. London: HMSO.

Blundell, R (1992), 'Labour supply and taxation: A survey', *Fiscal Studies*, 13(3), 15-40.

Bradshaw, J (ed.) (1993) *Household Budgets and Living Standards*. York: Joseph Rowntree Foundation.

Bradshaw, J and Millar, J (1991), *Lone Parent Families in the UK*, DSS Research Report No. 7. London: HMSO.

British Medical Journal (1993), *The Health of the Nation: The BMJ View*. London: BMJ.

Brown, J (1992), *A Policy Vacuum: Social security for the self-employed*. York: Joseph Rowntree Foundation.

Burchardt, T and Hills, J (1997) *Private Welfare Insurance and Social Security: Pushing the boundaries*. York: York Publishing Services.

Burghes, L (1993), *One-parent Families: Policy Options for the 1990s*. York: Joseph Rowntree Foundation.

Coleman, D (1989), 'The new housing policy: A critique', *Housing Studies*, 4(1), 44-57.

Commission on Social Justice (1994) *Social Justice: Strategies for National Renewal*. London: Vintage.

Department for Education [DfE] (1993), *Departmental Report*, Cm. 2210. London: HMSO.

Department for Education and Employment [DfEE] (1996) *Departmental Report*, Cm 2810. London: HMSO.

DfEE (1997) *Departmental Report*, Cm 3610. London: The Stationery Office.

Department of Health [DoH] (1989), *Caring for People: Community care in the next decade and beyond*, Cm. 849. London: HMSO.

DoH (1992), *The Health of the Nation*, Cm. 1986. London: HMSO.

DoH (1993), *Departmental Report*, Cm. 2212. London: HMSO.

DoH (1997) *Departmental Report*, Cm 3612. London: The Stationery Office.

Department of Social Security [DSS] (1991), *Options for Equality in State Pension Age*, Cm 1723. London: HMSO.

DSS (1993a), *Departmental Report*, Cm. 2213. London: HMSO.

DSS (1993b), *The Growth of Social Security*. London: HMSO.

DSS (1996a) *Households Below Average Incomes: A statitical analysis 1979-1993/94*. London: The Stationery Office.

DSS (1996b) *Social Security Statistics 1996*. London: The Stationery Office.

DSS (1997) *Social Security Departmental Report*, Cm 3613. London: The Stationery Office.

Department of the Environment [DoE] (1992a), *Competing for Quality in Housing*. London: DoE.

DoE (1992b), *Housing and Construction Statistics 1981-1991*. London: HMSO.

DoE (1993a), *Annual Report 1993*, Cm. 2207. London: HMSO.

DoE (1993b), *English House Condition Survey 1991*. London: HMSO.

DoE (1997) *Housing and Construction Statistics 1985-95*. London: The Stationery Office.

Dilnot, A and Johnson, P (1992), 'What pension should the state provide?', *Fiscal Studies*, 13(4), 1-20.

Dilnot, A, Kay, J and Morris, N (1984), *The Reform of Social Security*. Oxford: Oxford University Press.

Dorling, D. (1997) *Death in Britain: How local mortality rates have changed: 1950s-1990s*. York: Joseph Rowntree Foundation

Ermisch, J (1990), *Fewer Babies, Longer Lives*. York: Joseph Rowntree Foundation.

Esam, P and Berthoud, R (1991), *Independent Benefits for Men and Women*. London: Policy Studies Institute.

Evandrou, M (1992), 'Challenging the invisibility of carers: Mapping informal care nationally', in C Victor and F Lascko (eds), *Social Policy and Older People*. London: Gower.

Evandrou, M (1993), 'The health, employment and income status of informal carers in Britain', paper presented at British Society of Gerontology Annual Conference, Norwich.

Evandrou, M, Falkingham, J and Glennerster, H (1990), 'The personal social services: Everyone's poor relation and nobody's baby', in Hills (1990).

Evandrou, M, Falkingham, J, Hills, J and Le Grand, J (1993), 'Welfare benefits in kind and income distribution', *Fiscal Studies*, 14(1), 57-76.

Evandrou, M, Falkingham, J, Le Grand, J and Winter, D (1992), 'Equity in health and social care', *Journal of Social Policy*, 21(4), 489-523.

Evans, M and Glennerster, H (1993), 'Squaring the circle: The inconsistencies and constraints of Beveridge's Plan', Welfare State Programme Discussion Paper WSP/86. London: London School of Economics.

Falkingham, J (1989), 'Britain's ageing population: The engine behind increased dependency ratios', *Journal of Social Policy*, 18(2), 211-233.

Falkingham, J and Hills, J (1995) (eds), *The Dynamic of Welfare: The welfare state and the life cycle*. Hemel Hempstead: Harvester Wheatsheaf.

Falkingham, J, Hills, J and Lessof, C (1993), 'William Beveridge versus Robin Hood: Social security and redistribution over the lifecycle', Welfare State Programme Discussion Paper WSP/88. London: London School of Economics.

Falkingham, J and Johnson, P (1992), *Ageing and Economic Welfare*. London: Sage.

Falkingham, J and Johnson, P (1993), 'A unified pension scheme (UFPS) for Britain', Welfare State Programme Discussion Paper WSP/90. London: London School of Economics.

Feldstein, M S (1974), 'Social security, induced retirement and aggregate capital accumulation', *Journal of Political Economy*, 82, 905-926.

Field, F and Owen, M (1993), *Private Pensions for All: Squaring the circle*, Discussion Paper No.16. London: Fabian Society.

Garman, A, Redmond, G and Lonsdale, S (1992), *Incomes In and Out of Work: A cohort study of newly unemployed men and women*, DSS Research Report No. 7. London: HMSO.

Gibbs, I (1993), *Housing Wealth in Later Life: A mixed blessing*. York: Centre for Housing Policy, University of York.

Glennerster, H (1991), 'Quasi-markets and Education', *Economic Journal*, 101(1).

Glennerster, H and Evans, M (1994), 'Beveridge and his assumptive worlds: The incompatibilities of a flawed design', in Hills, Ditch and Glennerster (1994).

Glennerster, H and Low, W (1990), 'Education and the welfare state: Does it add up?', in Hills (1990).

Glennerster, H, Matsaganis, M and Owens, P (1994) *Implementing GP Fundholding: Wild card or winning hand?* Buckingham: Open University Press.

Bibliography

Government Actuary (1995) *National Insurance Fund: Long Term Financial Estimates*, HC (94-5) 160. London: HMSO.

Green, A and Steedman, H (1993), *Educational Provision, Educational Attachment and the Needs of Industry: A Review of Research for Germany, France, the USA and Britain*. London: NIESR.

Harris, J (1994), 'Beveridge's social and political thought', in Hills, Ditch and Glennerster (1994).

Hewitt, P (1993), *About Time*. London: IPPR.

Hills, J (1988), *Changing Tax: How the tax system works and how to change it*. London: CPAG Ltd.

Hills, J (1989), 'Counting the family silver: The public sector's balance sheet 1957 to 1987', *Fiscal Studies*, 10(2), 66-85.

Hills, J (1990) (ed.), *The State of Welfare: The welfare state in Britain since 1974*. Oxford: Clarendon Press.

Hills, J (1991a), *Unravelling Housing Finance: Subsidies, benefits and taxation*. Oxford: Clarendon Press.

Hills, J (1991b), *Thirty-nine Steps to Housing Finance Reform*. York: Joseph Rowntree Foundation.

Hills, J (1992), 'Does Britain have a "welfare generation"? An empirical analysis of intergenerational equity', Welfare State Programme Discussion Paper WSP/76. London: London School of Economics.

Hills, J (1995) *Income and Wealth Volume 2: A Summary of the evidence*. York: Joseph Rowntree Foundation.

Hills, J (1996) *New Inequalities: The changing distribution of income and wealth in the UK*. Cambridge: Cambridge University Press.

Hills, J, Ditch, J and Glennerster, H (1994), *Beveridge and Social Security: An international retrospective*. Oxford: Clarendon Press.

Hills, J and Mullings, B (1990), 'Housing: A decent home for all at a price within their means?', in Hills (1990).

HM Treasury (1997) *Public Expenditure: Statistical Analyses 1997-98*, Cm 3601. London: The Stationery Office.

Holtermann, S (1993), *Becoming a Breadwinner: Policies to assist lone parents with childcare*. London: Daycare Trust.

House of Commons Education Committee (1989), *First Report Session 1988/9*, HC(88-89)30-I. London: HMSO.

House of Commons Social Security Committee (1992), *Low Income Statistics: Low income families 1979-1989*, HC(92-93)359. London: HMSO.

House of Commons Social Security Committee (1995) *Low Income Statistics: Low income families 1989-92*, HC (94-5) 254. London: HMSO.

Illsley, R and Le Grand, J (1987), 'Measurement of inequality in health', in A Williams (ed.), *Economics and Health*. London: Macmillan.

Independent Working Group (chaired by Sir Alec Atkinson) (1993), *Pensions and Divorce*. London: Pensions Management Institute.

Inquiry into British Housing (1991), *Second Report*. York: Joseph Rowntree Foundation.

Irwin, S and Morris, L (1993), 'Social security or economic insecurity? The concentration of unemployment (and research) within households', *Journal of Social Policy*, 22(3), 349-372.

JRF Inquiry into Meeting the Costs of Continuing Care (1996) *Report*. York: Joseph Rowntree Foundation.

Kiernan, K and Estaugh, V (1993), *Cohabitation: Extra-marital childbearing and social policy*. London: Family Policy Studies Centre.

Kiernan, K and Wicks, M (1990), *Family Change and Future Policy*. York: Joseph Rowntree Foundation.

Kleinman, M and Whitehead, C (1992), *A Review of Housing Needs Assessment*. London: LSE Housing.

Le Grand, J (1993), *Quasi-markets and Community Care*. SAUS Studies in Decentralisation and Quasi-Markets No. 17. Bristol: School for Advanced Urban Studies.

Le Grand, J (1995) 'The market, the state and the distribution of lifecycle income' in Falkingham and Hills (1995).

Le Grand, J and Vizard, P (forthcoming) 'The National Health Service' in H Glennester and J Hills (eds), *The State of Welfare* (second edition). Oxford: Oxford University Press.

Le Grand, J and Illsley, R (1993), 'Regional inequalities in mortality', *Journal of Epidemiology and Community Health*.

Le Grand, J and Vizard, P (forthcoming) 'The National Health Service' in H Glennerster and J Hills (eds), *The State of Welfare* (second edition). Oxford: Oxford University Press.

Lewis, J and Glennerster, H (1996) *Implementing the New Community Care*. Buckingham: Open University Press

Marmor, T R, Mashaw, J L and Harvey, P L (1990), *America's Misunderstood Welfare State*. USA: Basic Books.
Marsh, A and McKay, S (1993), *Families, Work and Benefits*. London: Policy Studies Institute.

Meadows, P (1997) *The Integration of Taxes and Benefits for Working Families*. York: York Publishing Services.

Mitchell, B R (1988), *British Historical Statistics*. Cambridge: Cambridge University Press.

Murray, C (1984), *Losing Ground: American social policy 1950-1980*. New York: Basic Books.

Mulgan, G and Murray, R (1993), *Reconnecting Taxation*. London: Demos.

'No Turning Back' Group of Conservative MPs (1993), *Who Benefits? Reinventing social security*. London: Conservative Political Centre.

Oldman, C (1991), *Paying for Care: Personal sources of funding care*. York: Joseph Rowntree Foundation.

Organisation for Economic Co-operation and Development [OECD] (1985), *Social Expenditure 1960-1990: Problems of growth and control*. Paris: OECD.

OECD (1995) 'Effects of ageing populations on government budgets', *Economic Outlook*, June.

OECD (1996a) *Education at a Glance*. Paris: OECD.

OECD (1996b) *Social Expenditure Statistics of OECD Countries* (provisional). Paris: OECD.

Office for National Statistics (ONS) (1996) *Population Projections*, Series PP2, No 20. London: The Stationery Office.

ONS (1997a) *Economic Trends*, No 520, March.

ONS (1997b) *Living in Britain 1995: General Household Survey*. London: The Stationery Office.

Office of Population Censuses and Surveys [OPCS] (1981), *General Household Survey 1979*. London: HMSO.

OPCS (1993a) *General Household Survey 1991*. London: HMSO.

OPCS (1993b) *National population projections 1991-based*, series PP2, No. 18. London: HMSO.

Page, D (1993), *Building for Communities*. York: Joseph Rowntree Foundation.

Parker, H (1989), *Instead of the Dole*. London: Routledge.

Parker, H and Sutherland, H (1991), *Child Tax Allowances: A comparison of child benefits, child tax reliefs and basic incomes as instruments of family policy*, STICERD Occasional Paper No. 16. London: London School of Economics.

Piachaud, D (1993), *What's Wrong with Fabianism?*. London: Fabian Society.

Power, A (1993), *Hovels to High Rise: State housing in Europe since 1850*. London: Routledge.

Power, A (1997) *Estates on the Edge: The social consequences of mass housing in northern Europe*. London: Macmillan.

Robinson, R and Le Grand, J (eds) (1994) *Evaluating the NHS Reforms*. London: King's Fund Institute.

Roll, J (1991), *What is a Family? Benefit models and social realities*. London: Family Policy Studies Centre.

Roll, J (1992a), *Understanding Poverty: A guide to the concepts and measures*. London: Family Policy Studies Centre.

Roll, J (1992b), *Lone Parent Families in the European Community*. London: European Family and Social Policy Unit.

Saunders, P (1990), *A Nation of Home Owners*. London: Unwin Hyman.

Schorr, A (1992), *The Personal Social Services: An outside view*. York: Joseph Rowntree Foundation.

Sefton, T (1997) *The Changing Distribution of the Social Wage*, STICERD Occasional Paper 21. London: London School of Economics.

Snower, D (1992), 'The future of the welfare state', Discussion Paper in Economics No. 16/92. London: Birkbeck College.

Townsend, P and Davidson, N (1982), *Inequalities in Health: The Black Report*. Harmondsworth: Penguin.

Veit-Wilson, J (1994), 'Condemned to deprivation? Beveridge's responsibility for the invisibility of poverty', in Hills, Ditch and Glennerster (1994).

Waldfogel, J (1993), 'Women working for less: A longitudinal analysis of the family gap', Welfare State Programme Discussion Paper WSP/93. London: London School of Economics.

Webb, S (1994), 'Social insurance and poverty alleviation: An empirical analysis' in Baldwin and Falkingham (1994).

Webb, S and Wilcox, S (1991), *Time for Mortgage Benefits*. York: Joseph Rowntree Foundation.

Whitehead, M (1987), *The Health Divide: Inequalities in health in the 1980s*. London: Health Education Council.

Wilcox, S (1997), *Housing Finance Review 1997/8*. York: Joseph Rowntree Foundation.

Wilcox, S with Bramley, G, Ferguson, A, Perry, J and Woods, C (1993), *Local Housing Companies: New opportunities for council housing*. York: Joseph Rowntree Foundation.

Wilkinson R, (1996) *Unhealthy Societies*. London: Routledge.

Willetts, D (1993), *The Age of Enlightenment*. London: Social Market Foundation.

Yarrow, G (1993) *Social Security and Friendly Societies: Options for the future*. National Conference of Friendly Societies.